LOOK ONCE, LOOK AGAIN

Exploring Habitats

Written by
Marilyn Marks

Illustrated by
Laura Rader

Designed by
Moonhee Pak

Editor
Julie A. Baron

Project Director
Carolea Williams

Table of Contents

Introduction 3

LOOK-AT-A-BOOK ACTIVITIES

In the Desert

What's It Like to Be a Cactus? . . 5

Sensing the Desert 6

At the Zoo

Animal Puzzles 7

Various Vertebrates 10

At the Seashore

Paper-Bag Fish 13

Exploring a Tide Pool 16

In the Forest

Box Turtle 19

Forest Mural 21

In the Park

Miniature Parks 22

Whose Park Is It? 23

At the Pond

Dragonfly Data 24

Bullfrogs Everywhere 26

In the Meadow

Crazy Crawlers Competition . . 29

Slither Like a Snake 30

At the Farm

Holy Cow! 31

Silly Signs 35

In a Tree

Nifty Nests 36

Creating a Colorful Forest . . . 37

In the Garden

Fruits or Vegetables? 38

Mystery Plants 40

Among the Flowers

Petals 42

Flower Power 43

Underfoot

Ants, Ants Everywhere! 46

Earthworm Tunnels 48

USE-THE-CLUES ACTIVITIES

The Case of the Different Antennae . . 49

The Case of the Mysterious Smells . . . 52

The Secret of Plant Protection 54

Play the Animal Protection Game . . . 56

Feet Fossils 59

Mysterious Seeds 61

The Mystery of the Traveling Seeds . . 66

The Case of the Missing Teeth 69

Guess Who's Coming to Lunch 73

Wrap It Up Activities 75

Introduction

Exploring Habitats is the perfect companion to the *Look Once, Look Again* books for beginning readers. This resource guide provides a wealth of activities that correlate with the *Look Once, Look Again* books about habitats.

The *Look Once, Look Again* books invite children to explore a variety of habitats, such as the seashore and the forest, as well as the plants and animals that live in each habitat. Young readers explore up close such interesting aspects of nature as the "prolegs" of a caterpillar, the 22 fleshy tentacles of a star-nosed mole, the parachute seeds of a dandelion, and the beautiful "eyespots" of a peacock. Each individual book includes several "look once, look again" pages. A "look once" page presents a close-up photograph and clues to the identity of a "mystery photograph." Readers then turn to a "look again" page and see a "pulled-back" photograph of the entire image that reveals the close-up photo's identity. Fun and fascinating facts explain the "look again" photograph.

Collect the following *Look Once, Look Again* books to use with this activity guide.
In the Desert
At the Zoo
At the Seashore
✓*In the Forest*
✓*In the Park*
At the Pond
✓*In the Meadow*
At the Farm
✓*In a Tree*
✓*In the Garden*
✓*Among the Flowers*
✓*Underfoot*

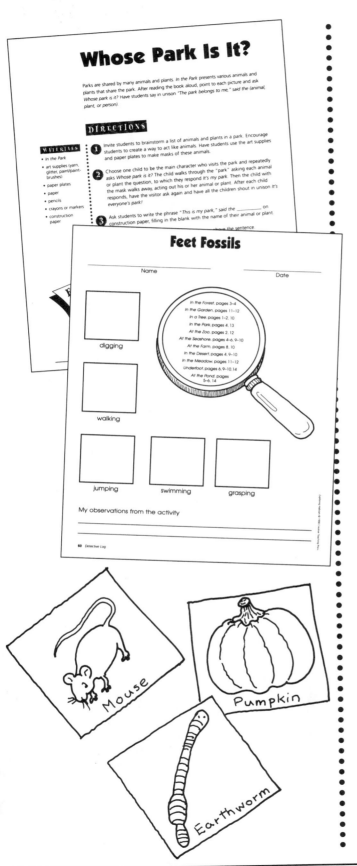

Exploring Habitats is divided into three activity sections. Activities in each section are science-based and include hands-on exploration, experiments, class books, dramatizations, graphs, art projects, and classification activities. Activity sections include the following:

LOOK-AT-A-BOOK ACTIVITIES

These engaging science activities apply to specific Look Once, Look Again books. Two activities are presented for each of the 12 books highlighted in this resource. Background information, a materials list, and easy-to-follow-instructions are provided for each activity.

USE-THE-CLUES ACTIVITIES

Children become detectives in a "detective agency" as they complete science activities that can be adapted for use with several of the Look Once, Look Again books. An individualized "detective log" is provided for each activity so students can record what they learn. The detective logs guide children in predicting outcomes, listing observations, and offering opinions.

WRAP IT UP ACTIVITIES

Wrap It Up activities incorporate the use of the animal and plant cut-outs on pages 77–80. These activities are a fun way to extend the learning from the previous sections of the book, and make perfect culminating or "take a break" activities. Suggestions are also provided for incorporating the fun facts that are included with each activity.

Your students' interest in and knowledge of science will grow as they participate in the meaningful activities provided in this resource. Exploring Habitats gives you everything you need to make science "come alive" for your students.

What's It Like to Be a Cactus?

Cacti are very important to animals that live in a desert. Insects, birds, and other small animals eat cacti for nourishment. Other animals live inside the stems of larger plants. After reading aloud *In the Desert*, have students discuss what it might be like to be a cactus. Then ask them to think about their feelings as they create their own cactus.

DIRECTIONS

MATERIALS

- *In the Desert*
- varieties of cacti
- 8 ½" x 11" (21.5 cm x 28 cm) cardboard
- glue
- sand
- writing paper
- tray
- green modeling clay or salt dough
- toothpicks or abaca plant material (available at craft stores)

1 Have students observe several types of cacti and notice size, flowers, and shape. Caution students not to touch the plants and observe with their eyes only.

2 Have students draw a horizontal line to divide a piece of cardboard in half. Students should then spread glue over the top half, sprinkle sand onto the glue, and shake the excess sand into the tray. Have the children glue writing paper to the bottom half and write a short rhyme describing the cactus.

3 Ask each student to form a small ball of modeling clay into one or more cactus plants.

4 Have children make spines by poking the clay with a toothpick or by inserting small pieces of abaca into the clay. Attach the cactus to the sandy part of the paper.

Fun Facts

- A cactus over 57 feet tall was found in Arizona! That's taller than a five-story building.
- Imagine eating a peanut butter and jelly sandwich made from a cactus. Believe it or not, some cacti produce fruit that is made into jelly.
- As early as 1929, Arizona passed laws protecting cacti from thieves who would dig them up and sell them to flower shops.

Sensing the Desert

Many animals have more highly developed senses than humans have. These senses help animals find food and stay safe. Read aloud *In the Desert* and ask children how each animal described uses its senses. For example, the gecko uses its sense of sight to hunt for food. Use the following activity to give students practice in using their senses.

DIRECTIONS

MATERIALS

- *In the Desert*
- paper lunch bags
- small objects (paper clip, eraser, chalk, crayon, ruler, Scratch 'N Sniff stickers, hole punch)
- science journal

1 Have each student secretly place a small object inside a lunch bag and close the top.

2 Divide the class into pairs and have each pair exchange paper bags.

3 Have students shake the bag and then write down in a science journal predictions about the bag's contents.

4 Instruct students to smell the bags and record any further clues.

5 Encourage students to touch the outside of the bag and see if they can determine the identity of the object. Have them record in their journals any further observations.

6 Finally, have them close their eyes, reach inside, and hold the object. Ask students to record their final observations and predict the identity of the object. Invite students to look inside and check their predictions.

7 Discuss the senses that were used to complete this experiment.

Fun Facts

- The desert fox has large ears that help it stay cool in the hot desert sun.
- A rattlesnake has a special heat-sensing pit on its head. The pit can detect heat given off by rabbits and other warm-blooded prey.
- Did you know that the kangaroo rat can live in the desert without ever taking a drink of water? It gets enough water from the plant seeds it eats.

Animal Puzzles

People are used to seeing animals at the zoo but rarely do they get to see them in their natural habitat. Not all animals can be found on all continents. After reading aloud *At the Zoo*, find out where the animals in the book come from. For example, lions, such as the one on page 6, can be found on the African continent. Encourage children to notice that the descriptions of most animals give hints as to where in the wild the animals can be found.

DIRECTIONS

MATERIALS

- *At the Zoo*
- tracing paper
- pencil
- Zoo Animals reproducible (page 9)
- masking tape
- large craft sticks
- markers or colored pencils (optional)

1 Have each student trace onto tracing paper one animal from the Zoo Animals reproducible.

2 Instruct students to lay six craft sticks in a row and tape the ends down.

3 Have students place the tracing paper (picture side down) onto the craft sticks and rub the pencil lead over the tracing paper to transfer the drawing.

4 Tell students to remove the tracing paper and use the pencil to accentuate the details of the animal.

Animal Puzzles

5 Encourage students to color the animal with markers or colored pencils. Have them write the animal's name and continent on the bottom craft stick. Remind students to look in the book for clues about this information.

Tiger–Asia

6 Invite students to remove the masking tape.

7 Have students pair up and swap puzzles. Store puzzles in a resealable plastic bag.

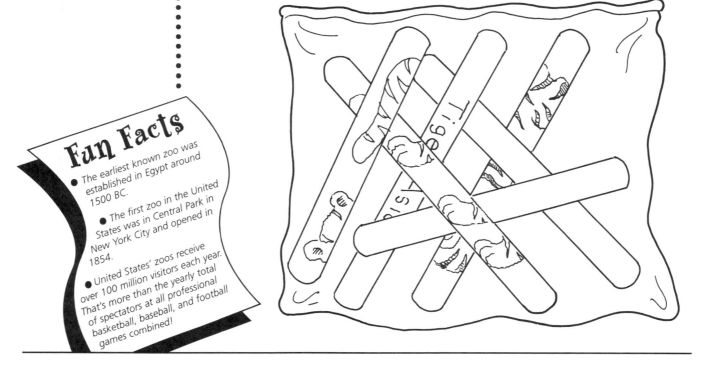

Fun Facts

● The earliest known zoo was established in Egypt around 1500 BC.

● The first zoo in the United States was in Central Park in New York City and opened in 1854.

● United States' zoos receive over 100 million visitors each year. That's more than the yearly total of spectators at all professional basketball, baseball, and football games combined!

Zoo Animals

Tiger

Amazon Parrot

Camel

Zebra

Elephant

Lion

Various Vertebrates

Animals with backbones can be sorted into five classes: fish, amphibians, reptiles, birds, and mammals. *At the Zoo* presents examples of birds and mammals. After reading the book aloud, ask students to tell if each animal pictured has fur/hair or feathers. Explain that scientists sort animals into groups based on these characteristics and others. The following activity helps students classify vertebrates.

DIRECTIONS

MATERIALS

- *At the Zoo*
- Animal Sort reproducible (page 12)

1 Divide the class into pairs. Have each pair color and cut out each animal card on the Animal Sort reproducible.

2 Ask students to sort the cards into groups based on the animals' characteristics. Then have them share their reasons for sorting the cards the way they did.

3 Explain that scientists group animals into the following categories:

Fish—internal skeleton; live in water; body covered with wet scales; cold-blooded; breathe with gills; most lay eggs (sunfish).

Amphibians—internal skeleton; moist skin; undergo metamorphosis; cold-blooded; breathe with gills when young and with lungs as adults; lay soft eggs in the water (frog, newt, salamander).

Reptiles—internal skeleton; live in water and/or on land; body covered with dry scales; cold-blooded; breathe with lungs; lay leathery-shelled eggs (snake, snapping turtle, crocodile).

Birds—internal skeleton; body covered with feathers; warm-blooded; breathe with lungs; lay hard-shelled eggs (parrot, peacock, kingfisher, duck, swan).

Mammals—internal skeleton; body covered with hair; warm-blooded; breathe with lungs; young are born alive (tiger, lion, elephant, camel, zebra).

Various Vertebrates

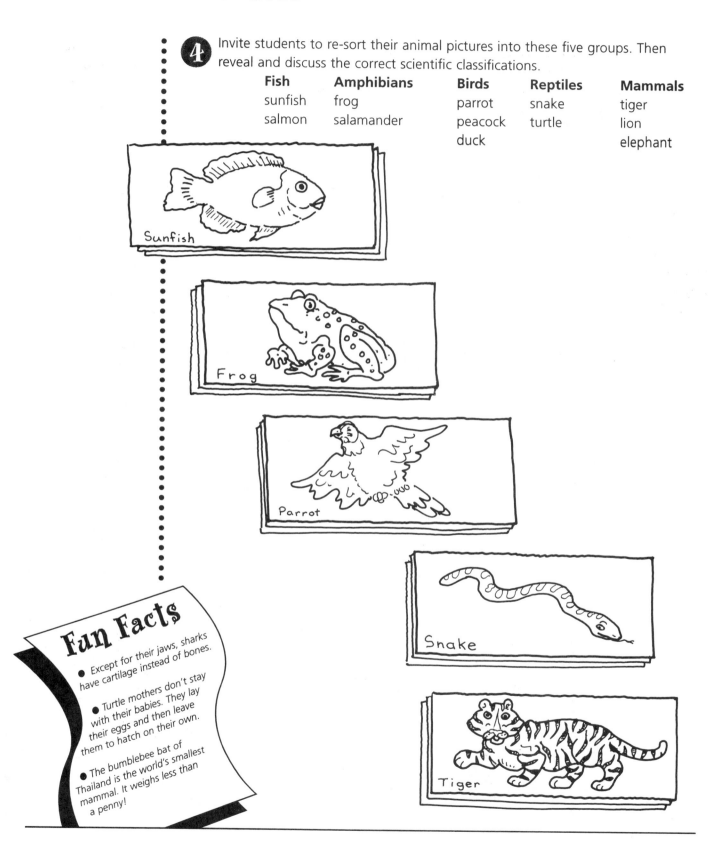

4 Invite students to re-sort their animal pictures into these five groups. Then reveal and discuss the correct scientific classifications.

Fish	Amphibians	Birds	Reptiles	Mammals
sunfish	frog	parrot	snake	tiger
salmon	salamander	peacock	turtle	lion
		duck		elephant

Sunfish

Frog

Parrot

Snake

Tiger

Fun Facts

● Except for their jaws, sharks have cartilage instead of bones.

● Turtle mothers don't stay with their babies. They lay their eggs and then leave them to hatch on their own.

● The bumblebee bat of Thailand is the world's smallest mammal. It weighs less than a penny!

Animal Sort

Turtle

Peacock

Duck

Salamander

Lion

Elephant

Sunfish

Snake

Frog

Parrot

Tiger

Salmon

Exploring Habitats © 1998 Creative Teaching Press

Paper-Bag Fish

One animal that the book *At the Seashore* takes a look at is the sea urchin, and it explains how sea urchins travel by moving their spines back and forth. Discuss how people move. Tell students that they will be studying how another sea creature, the fish, travels. Using the Fish Diagram, discuss the various parts of a fish and encourage students to guess the function of each part. Explain that fish use their tails to swim and their fins to balance and steer.

DIRECTIONS

MATERIALS

- *At the Seashore*
- Fish Diagram (page 14)
- Fin reproducible (page 15)
- lunch bag
- cellophane tape
- rubber band
- crayons or markers
- ½ sheets of newspaper
- construction paper/tagboard
- stapler

1 Have students fold down the corners of the bag bottom and tape them in place.

2 Encourage students to color both sides of the fish the same color and include eyes, gill flaps, scales, and a mouth.

3 Ask students to color the fin patterns and cut them out.

4 Staple the dorsal fin between the bag folds at the top of the fish. Have children tape other fins to the appropriate places.

5 Instruct students to stuff the "body" with newspaper and secure the open end with a rubber band about 3" (7.5 cm) from the end. Have students fan out the end of the bag to make a tail.

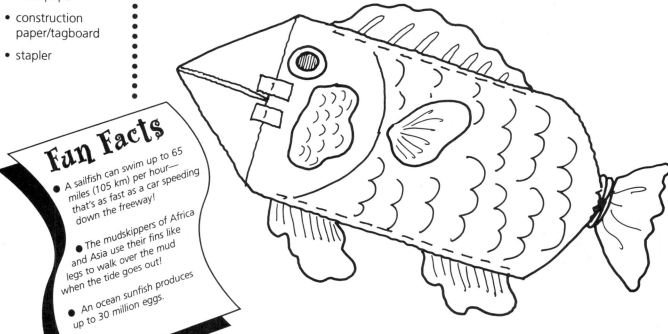

Fun Facts
- A sailfish can swim up to 65 miles (105 km) per hour—that's as fast as a car speeding down the freeway!
- The mudskippers of Africa and Asia use their fins like legs to walk over the mud when the tide goes out!
- An ocean sunfish produces up to 30 million eggs.

Fish Diagram

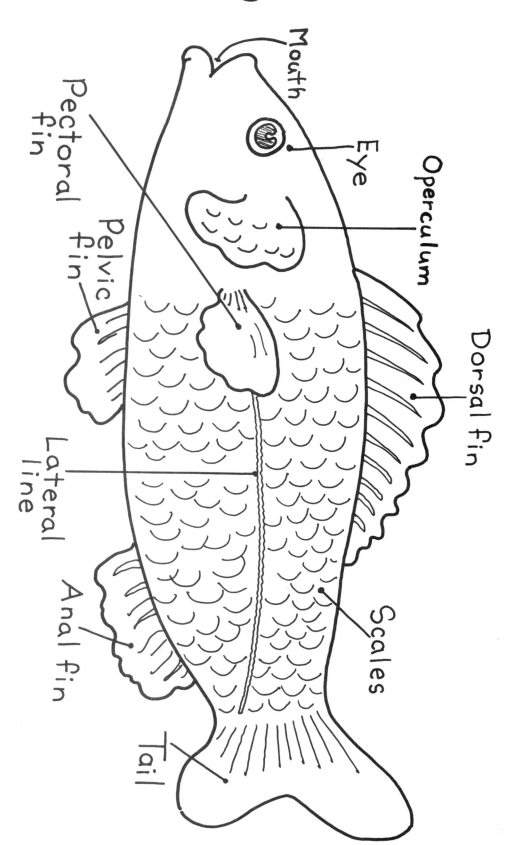

Mouth

Eye

Operculum

Pectoral fin

Pelvic fin

Dorsal fin

Lateral line

Scales

Anal fin

Tail

Fins

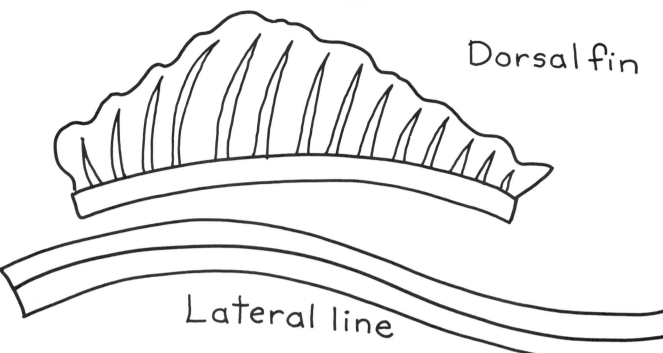

Dorsal fin

Lateral line

Operculum

Pelvic fin

Anal fin

Pectoral fin

Exploring a Tide Pool

Tide pools are fun and interesting places for exploring and studying sea life. During high tide, hermit crabs and barnacles are visible; during low tide, starfish and sea urchins can be observed.

DIRECTIONS

MATERIALS

- *At the Seashore*
- Exploring a Tide Pool reproducible (page 18)
- 11" x 17" (28 cm x 43 cm) tagboard or light cardboard
- 1 ½" x 12" (4 cm x 30.5 cm) tagboard strips
- one of each of the following strips of blue construction paper:

    10 ½" x 4 ½" (26 cm x 11 cm) (wave)

    1" x 5" (2.5 cm x 12.5 cm) (handle for wave)

    11" x 3 ½" (28 cm x 9 cm) (ocean)

- crayons
- glue
- masking tape

1 Have students color the Exploring a Tide Pool reproducible.

2 Ask students to glue the 11" x 3 ½" (28 cm x 9 cm) strip of blue construction paper to the bottom of the tagboard to represent the ocean. Have students glue the Exploring a Tide Pool reproducible directly above it.

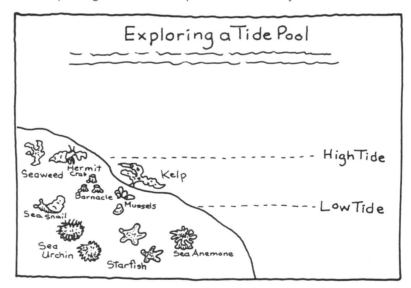

3 Have students tape two 1 ½" x 12" (4 cm x 30.5 cm) tagboard strips along the side to create pockets.

Exploring a Tide Pool

4 Have students create a "wave" by cutting curvy wave shapes into the 10 ½" x 4 ½" (26 cm x 11 cm) piece of blue construction paper. Instruct them to tape the small strip of construction paper to the back of the wave to serve as a handle.

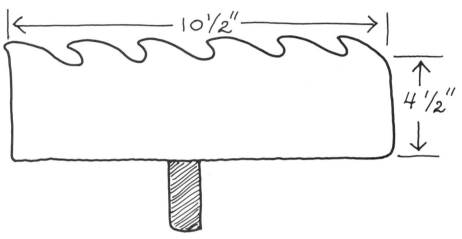

5 Invite students to slide the "wave" into the pockets and use the handle to pull down the "wave" to simulate high tide and low tide.

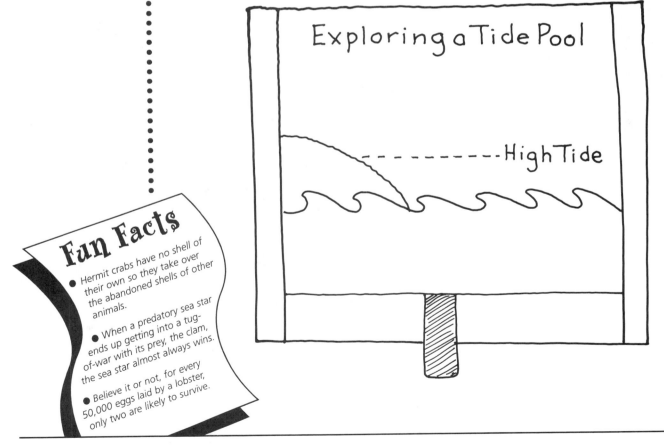

Fun Facts

- Hermit crabs have no shell of their own so they take over the abandoned shells of other animals.

- When a predatory sea star ends up getting into a tug-of-war with its prey, the clam, the sea star almost always wins.

- Believe it or not, for every 50,000 eggs laid by a lobster, only two are likely to survive.

Exploring a Tide Pool

When the tide goes out, we can see many plants and animals that live near the shore. Pull the water down slowly to see what lives in a tide pool.

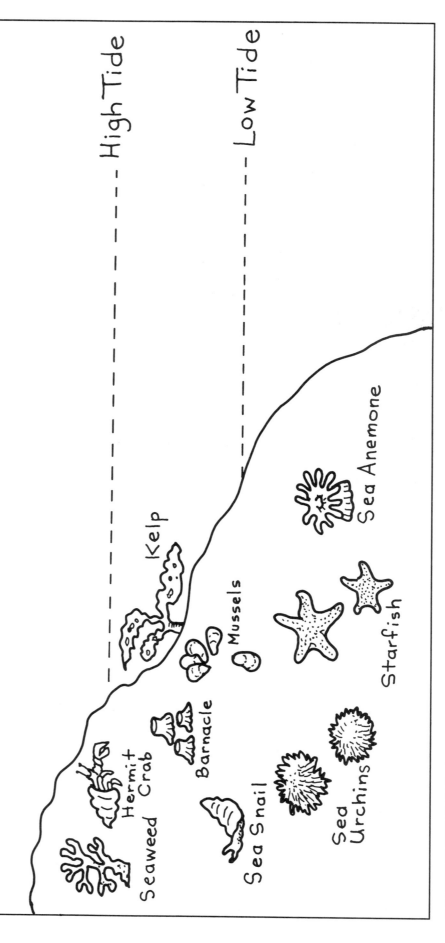

High Tide

Low Tide

Kelp

Mussels

Sea Anemone

Starfish

Hermit Crab

Barnacle

Seaweed

Sea Snail

Sea Urchins

Exploring Habitats © 1998 Creative Teaching Press

Box Turtle

The box turtle gets its name from its ability to withdraw inside its shell and look like a box. The box turtle, like most other land turtles, has a high dome-shaped shell and scaly legs. After reading aloud *In the Forest*, have students discuss the details they noticed on the turtle. For example, the photographed turtle has scaly feet with claws at the ends of its toes. Remind students to remember these features when they make their own turtles.

DIRECTIONS

1. Have students observe the photograph of a box turtle on page 4 of *In the Forest*. Discuss the lifestyle of the turtle, such as what it eats and how it walks.

2. Give each student a paper plate, ½ of a tennis ball or Styrofoam ball, a piece of wax paper, green modeling clay (about the size of a tennis ball), and brown modeling clay (about the size of a Ping-Pong ball).

3. Have students use the green modeling clay to make a 4"-diameter (10 cm) "pancake."

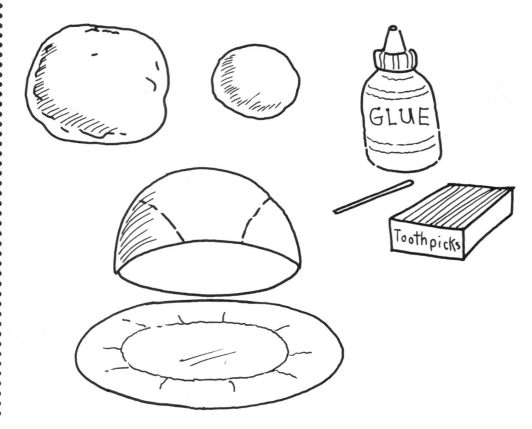

Box Turtle

4 Instruct students to put several drops of glue on the outside of the ball. Have students drape the clay pancake over the ball and press it gently in place.

5 Have students glue the rim of the ball to the center of the plate.

6 Have students make a head, four feet, and a tail from brown modeling clay and glue them in position.

7 Have students use a toothpick to make eyes, a mouth, and scales on the shell to complete their turtles.

Fun Facts

● Imagine burying yourself in the dirt to cool off! This is one way a turtle cools off because it doesn't have sweat glands.

● A turtle's heart rate is 20–30 beats per minute compared to a human heart rate, which is about 70 beats per minute.

● Did you know that box turtles can live to be 100 years old? No wonder their skin is so wrinkly!

Forest Mural

All forests have five parts. The *canopy* is overhead and is made up of the tallest treetops. Under the canopy is the *understory*. The understory is made up of shorter trees than those forming the canopy. The *shrub layer* is under the understory while ferns and wildflowers can be found in the *herb layer* below the shrubs. The *forest floor* is the "lowest" layer and is like the garbage can of the forest. Overripe fruit, fallen leaves, and dead animals are often deposited there.

DIRECTIONS

MATERIALS

- *In the Forest*
- butcher paper
- tempera paints/brushes
- pencils (optional)

1 After reading aloud the book *In the Forest*, have children name the plants and animals discussed in the book.

2 Explain that a forest has five layers: canopy, understory, shrub layer, herb layer, and forest floor.

3 Have children create a mural that depicts the five layers of the forest.

4 Challenge children to think of animals that would live in the forest and at which layer they would live. Encourage them to draw or paint the animals in the appropriate places.

5 Have children color leaves and staple the leaf tops over the animals to provide camouflage that can be lifted to reveal a hidden creature.

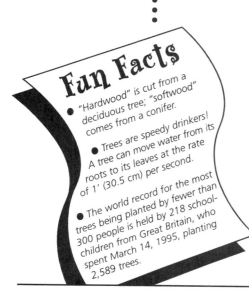

Fun Facts

- "Hardwood" is cut from a deciduous tree; "softwood" comes from a conifer.
- Trees are speedy drinkers! A tree can move water from its roots to its leaves at the rate of 1' (30.5 cm) per second.
- The world record for the most trees being planted by fewer than 300 people is held by 218 school-children from Great Britain, who spent March 14, 1995, planting 2,589 trees.

Miniature Parks

Parks are wonderful places to go to relax and *In the Park* presents a beautiful example. After reading the book aloud, ask children to share some experiences they have had at a park and name some things that they found there. Discuss how a park is maintained. Then have students design their ideal park.

DIRECTIONS

MATERIALS

- *In the Park*
- soda-can box bottoms
- plastic wrap
- potting soil
- grass seed
- craft supplies (pipe cleaners, craft sticks, clay, glue)
- science journal

1 Have small groups of students line soda-can box bottoms with plastic wrap and fill them with potting soil.

2 Instruct students to plant the grass seed.

3 Encourage the groups to design the perfect park and use the craft supplies to make playground equipment, picnic tables, and benches for their miniature park.

4 Direct the groups to create a maintenance schedule for the miniature park and include this in their science journals. This should include watering and lawn-mowing schedules.

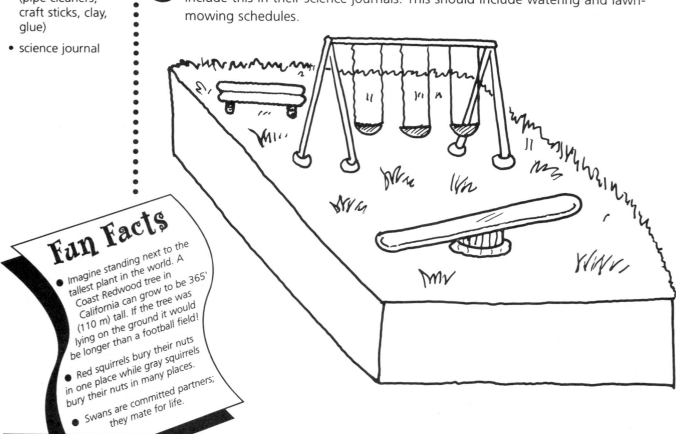

Fun Facts

- Imagine standing next to the tallest plant in the world. A Coast Redwood tree in California can grow to be 365' (110 m) tall. If the tree was lying on the ground it would be longer than a football field!

- Red squirrels bury their nuts in one place while gray squirrels bury their nuts in many places.

- Swans are committed partners; they mate for life.

Whose Park Is It?

Parks are shared by many animals and plants. *In the Park* presents various animals and plants that share the park. After reading the book aloud, point to each picture and ask *Whose park is it?* Have students say in unison *"The park belongs to me,"* said the (animal, plant, or person).

DIRECTIONS

MATERIALS

- *In the Park*
- art supplies (yarn, glitter, paint/paint-brushes)
- paper plates
- paper
- pencils
- crayons or markers
- construction paper

1 Invite students to brainstorm a list of animals and plants in a park. Encourage students to create a way to act like animals. Have students use the art supplies and paper plates to make masks of these animals.

2 Choose one child to be the main character who visits the park and repeatedly asks *Whose park is it?* The child walks through the "park" asking each animal or plant the question, to which they respond *It's my park*. Then the child with the mask walks away, acting out his or her animal or plant. After each child responds, have the visitor ask again and have all the children shout in unison *It's everyone's park!*

3 Ask students to write the phrase *"This is my park,"* said the _____ on construction paper, filling in the blank with the name of their animal or plant.

4 Inspire children to color a corresponding picture above the sentence.

5 Compile pages in a class book titled *Whose Park Is It?* On the last page of the book write *Whose park is it? It's everyone's park!* Bind the pages and place the book in the classroom library.

Fun Facts

- The largest national park in the world is the National Park of Northeastern Greenland, which covers 375,289 sq. miles (600,462 sq. km). Imagine having to mow the grass!

- Boston Commons was the first park in the United States. It opened in 1634.

- Grass has a fibrous root system which, unlike the tap root, spreads out in all directions.

"This is my park," said the raccoon.

It's my park.

Dragonfly Data

Dragonflies have enormous eyes. After reading the book aloud, ask students to discuss facts about the dragonfly. Explain that they are going to make a model of this fascinating insect and learn about its body parts.

DIRECTIONS

MATERIALS

- *At the Pond*
- Wing Pattern (page 25)
- manila tagboard or cardstock
- flat doll clothespins
- 4" (10 cm) pieces of black pipe cleaner
- floral tape
- ½" diameter sequins
- black marker
- staple gun

1 Copy the Wing Pattern onto manila tagboard or cardstock.

2 Have students color the round "head" and curved "thorax" (middle section) of the clothespin with black marker.

3 Have students wrap one pipe cleaner around the head to create the antennae.

4 Instruct students to wrap floral tape around the remainder of the clothespin.

5 Invite children to cut out wings and draw veins on both sides.

6 Use the staple gun to carefully staple three pieces of pipe cleaner under the "thorax." Once bent in half, these will serve as legs.

7 Tell students to glue the wings over the black "thorax" section.

8 Have students glue on sequin "compound eyes" onto either side of the round head.

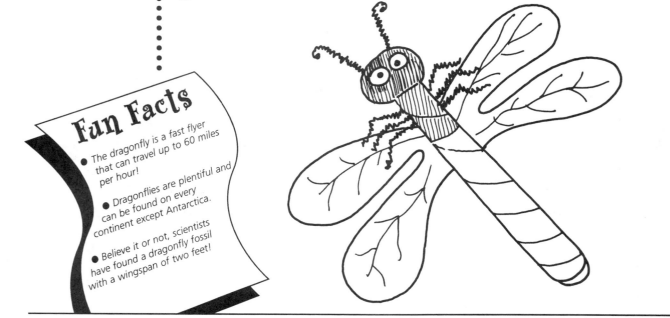

Fun Facts
- The dragonfly is a fast flyer that can travel up to 60 miles per hour!
- Dragonflies are plentiful and can be found on every continent except Antarctica.
- Believe it or not, scientists have found a dragonfly fossil with a wingspan of two feet!

Wing Pattern

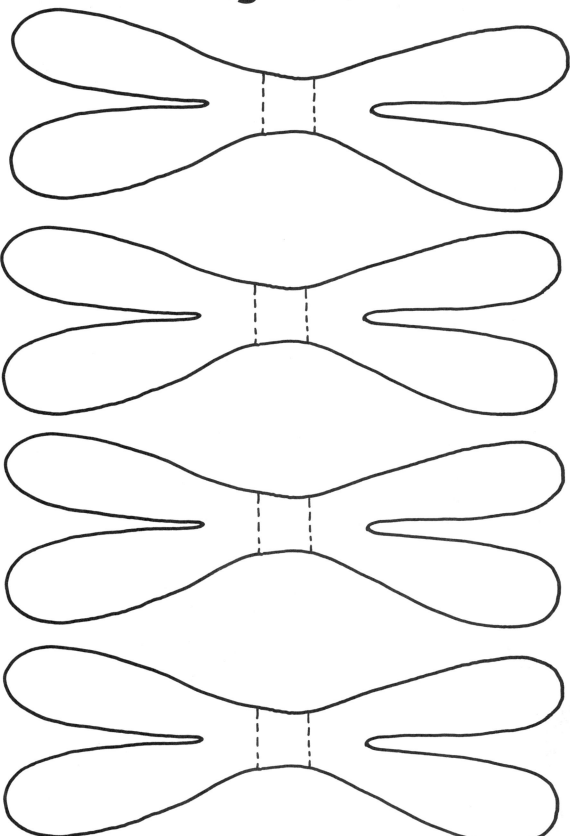

Bullfrogs Everywhere

At the Pond discusses how a bullfrog searches for insects and shoots out its long, sticky tongue to catch them. Ask students to demonstrate this with their tongues. Discuss how a frog's tongue is different from a human tongue. (A frog's tongue is attached to the front of its mouth.) Explain that, with this project, students will be simulating the way a frog catches insects.

DIRECTIONS

MATERIALS

- *At the Pond*
- Bullfrogs reproducible (page 27)
- 5 ½" (14 cm) x 8 ½" (21 cm) tagboard or cardstock
- craft sticks
- scissors
- crayons
- masking tape
- glue
- roll-up blower party favor
- Ten Speckled Frogs (page 28)

1 Copy the Bullfrog reproducible onto tagboard or cardstock.

2 Have each student color and cut out a frog.

3 Tell students to tape a craft stick to the frog back to make a puppet handle.

4 Have students cut slits at the X. Invite students to insert the party favor mouthpiece into the slit and tape it in place.

5 Encourage students to hold the frog by the craft stick handle and blow into the party favor to simulate the extension of the frog's tongue when catching insects.

6 Have students recite *Ten Speckled Frogs* and act out "catching flies." After the line *And then he jumped*, have students blow the "tongue."

Fun Facts

- In frog competitions, jumps are measured by the total distance in three leaps. The longest frog jump recorded measured 33 feet 5 ½"(10 m)!

- Frogs need to keep moist, but they don't drink water like humans; instead they "drink" water through their skin.

- A group of frogs is called an "army."

Bullfrogs

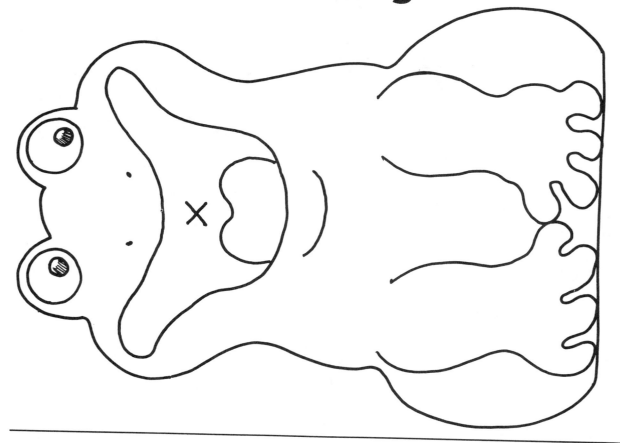

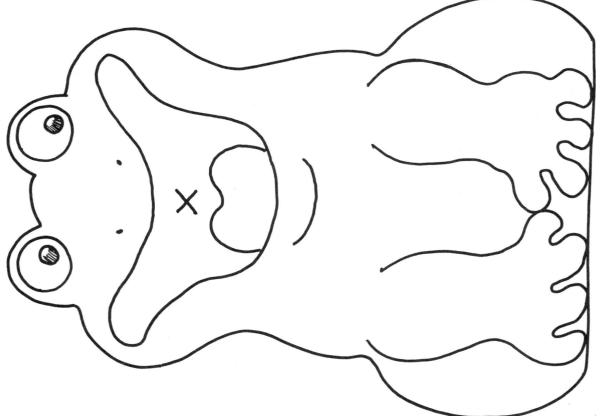

Ten Speckled Frogs

There were ten speckled frogs
Who sat on a log
By the edge of the pool,
Getting ready for school.

The little one said,
"I haven't been fed
I'm hungry...
I'm hungry..."

He spied a fly
Just passing by
And then he jumped
And went kerplunkt!

There were nine...eight...and so on.

Last Verse

He spied a fly
Just passing by
And then he jumped
Got it! Gulumph!

Reprinted with permission from Newbridge Educational Publishing, 1997.

Exploring Habitats © 1998 Creative Teaching Press

Crazy Crawlers Competition

Sometimes people mistake spiders for insects. Spiders are arachnids and differ from grasshoppers, which are insects. After reading aloud *In the Meadow*, ask children to compare the spider and grasshopper pictured. Have students compare eyes, body segments, and legs. Point out that spiders have eight legs, eight simple eyes, two body segments, and no antennae. Grasshoppers have six legs, two compound eyes, three body segments and two antennae. In this game, students will use the craft supplies in a race to make either a spider or an insect.

DIRECTIONS

MATERIALS

- *In the Meadow*
- six-sided die
- glue
- craft supplies (drinking straws, craft sticks, wiggly eyes, Styrofoam balls)
- writing paper

1 Form groups of 3–4 students. Give each group glue, craft sticks, and other craft supplies.

2 List the following attributes with the corresponding die on the board:

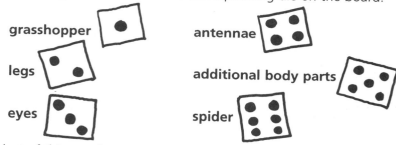

grasshopper

legs

eyes

antennae

additional body parts

spider

3 The object of this race is to create a crazy crawler (either an insect or spider) by rolling the die and adding the body parts that correspond to that number on the die. Each child begins with one body segment. First a child must roll a one or a six to determine which creature he or she will create. If a child rolls a two, she or he gets to use the craft supplies to add the legs. If a child rolls a number twice, he or she loses that turn. The game continues until everyone has created a new crazy crawler.

4 When finished, have students identify their creature as either a spider or an insect and write a four-line rhyme on the writing paper describing it.

For example: My spider crawls up and down,
With two body parts furry and brown.
It has eight legs and eight eyes too.
I wonder if it'll sneak up and bite you!

Fun Facts

- Grasshoppers can jump as far as 30 inches!
- Some spiders can jump 40 times their body length. If a five-foot-tall student could jump like that, he or she would be able to jump over five school buses lined up.
- The African sun spider can reach speeds of 10 mph!

Slither Like a Snake

Have students look at the beautiful green snake on page 8 of *In the Meadow*. Ask students to name ways a snake's body is different from their body. For example, snakes don't have legs or ears, their bodies are covered with scales, and their body shape is different from the students'. Explain that they will explore how a snake travels with no legs.

DIRECTIONS

MATERIALS

• *In the Meadow*

1 Have students explore the various ways they can move without walking, including rolling, spinning, and scooting.

2 Encourage students to feel their ribs and backbone while trying to move from side to side. While standing, demonstrate how to lift the chest and ribs by hunching over and then arching the back. Explain that this motion simulates the movements of a snake.

3 Invite students to lie on the floor and see if they can move and slither like a snake.

4 Ask questions such as *How easy was it to move like a snake?* and *Is there anything that would make slithering easier?*

5 Have children try to move like other animals pictured in the book. For example, they could crawl like a spider, hide like a fawn, and hop like a grasshopper.

Fun Facts

• Unlike other reptiles, snakes have no eyelids!

• Imagine being able to eat a whole hamburger in one bite! A snake can. It doesn't chew its food. It unhinges its jaw and swallows the food whole!

• If you try to outrun the black mamba, you'd better be in good shape. This snake can reach speeds of 10–12 miles per hour!

Holy Cow!

Farm animals need a farmer to take care of them. After reading aloud *At the Farm*, discuss each pictured animal and talk about what it needs to live. Explain that while caring for the animals costs a lot of money, profits are also made. This activity helps children calculate math problems associated with raising cows.

DIRECTIONS

MATERIALS

- *At the Farm*
- paper
- pencils
- 18 cards with either an *X* or an *O* (nine of each)
- Cow Questions reproducible (pages 33-34)
- happy face/unhappy face cards

1 Introduce a version of tic-tac-toe in which a player can place an *X* or *O* on a human grid only after answering a question correctly. Each person should have a pencil and scrap paper to calculate answers.

2 Choose nine people to be the "squares" and two others to be the *X* and *O* (contestants).

    a. Give each square one *X* and one *O* card.

    b. Distribute the happy face/unhappy face cards to each of the remaining students.

    c. Flip a coin to decide which contestant goes first. The first contestant chooses a square by calling a student's name.

    d. When a square is chosen, ask a question from the cow questions and have the square give an answer.

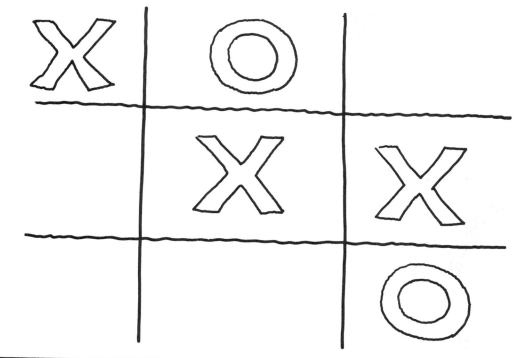

Holy Cow!

e. The children who are still at their seats raise either a happy face card to show agreement or an unhappy face card to show disagreement.

f. The first contestant then answers Agree or Disagree. If the contestant's answer is correct, the player receives an *X* or *O* by having the student in the square hold up the appropriate letter for the rest of the game.

g. Continue playing until one contestant gets a tic-tac-toe by agreeing or disagreeing correctly with three squares in a row.

Fun Facts

● A farmer can positively identify a cow through a "fingerprint" of its nose!

● The United States produces the most cheese in the world—over 6.5 billion pounds annually. This averages to 26 pounds per person per year.

● Joseph Love of Kenya holds the world's hand-milking record of 117 gallons from 30 cows on August 25, 1992.

Cow Questions

1 If a dairy cow weighs 1,400 pounds, how much would 2 such cows weigh? (2,800 pounds)

2 If a dairy cow weighs 1,400 pounds and a car weighs 2,000 pounds, what is the difference in weight? (600 pounds)

3 If a dairy cow weighs 1,400 pounds, how much would 4 cows of that weight weigh? (5,600 pounds)

4 If I had a herd of 49 dairy cows on my farm and 16 got lost, how many would still be on the farm? (33 cows)

5 If a cow can produce 7 gallons of milk each day, how much milk can she produce in 3 days? (21 gallons)

6 If a cow produces 7 gallons of milk but 2 gallons spill on the floor, how much milk will still be in the bucket? (5 gallons)

7 If a cow can produce enough milk to make 6 pounds of cheese, how much cheese would the milk from 4 such cows make? (24 pounds)

8 If you have 16 ounces of cheese and you use 7 ounces of cheese to make a casserole, how much cheese will be left for tomorrow's dinner? (9 ounces)

9 If two cows produce enough milk to make 5 pounds of butter, how much butter will the milk from 6 such cows make? (15 pounds)

Cow Questions

10 My brother went to the store and bought 6 pounds of butter. My father sent him back to get 3 more pounds. How much butter did my brother buy altogether? (9 pounds)

11 Each day, a farmer spends $3.50 to feed a cow. How much would that farmer spend on one cow for a whole week? ($24.50)

12 If it costs a farmer $3.50 to feed one cow, how much will it cost to feed 4 cows? ($14.00)

13 Pretend that you went to your favorite hamburger stand and bought your favorite meal for $4.75. It costs a farmer $3.50 to feed a cow for a day. What is the difference in cost between your meal and the cow's food? ($1.25)

14 A cow drinks 30 gallons of water each day. How much water would 5 such cows drink? (150 gallons)

15 A cow eats 20 pounds of grain and 35 pounds of silage each day. How many pounds of food does the cow eat in one day? (55 pounds) In two days? (110 pounds)

16 Each day, it costs a farmer $3.50 to feed a cow, $2.75 to give it shelter, and $1.25 for other supplies. How much does it cost altogether? ($7.50)

17 A cow drinks 30 gallons of water in one day. It is recommended that people drink 1 gallon of water each day. What is the difference between how much a cow drinks and how much a person drinks? (29 gallons)

Exploring Habitats © 1998 Creative Teaching Press

Silly Signs

Animals have unique features that we associate with each type. For example, when asked to think of an elephant feature, most people would probably say *trunk*. After reading aloud *At the Farm*, discuss the unique features of each type of animal in the book. Then invite students to play Silly Signs to demonstrate the features.

DIRECTIONS

MATERIALS

• *At the Farm*

1 Discuss farms and animals found there.

2 Divide the class into circles of 8–10 students. Each circle plays its own game.

3 Have each student choose a different farm animal and create a "sign" to represent that animal. For example, a student may demonstrate a cow by making a milking motion and saying *moo*. Once students have created a sign, each student shows the sign to the rest of the group.

4 Choose one person to start. That person shows his or her sign and then the sign of another person. This other person must be paying attention and see his or her sign. Once the second player sees his or her sign, the second player responds by showing it and shows the sign of a third person. This continues until someone misses his or her sign. Whenever a person misses his or her sign, he or she is eliminated from the game. The game continues until only two people remain. Then the game begins again.

Fun Facts

• On one acre of land, you will find approximately 360 million insects!

• Other than people, pigs are the only mammals that can get sunburned.

• The largest hog on record was Big Bill. He weighed 2,552 pounds when he died in 1933!

Nifty Nests

Everyone needs shelter to survive. Brainstorm with children the types of shelter that various animals call home. After reading aloud *In a Tree*, ask students about the type of home birds build and what materials they use (such as twigs, grass, hair, and plant fibers). Encourage students to name body parts birds use to help them build nests. Then have students pretend to be birds and build their own nests.

DIRECTIONS

MATERIALS

- *In a Tree*
- twigs, grass, and other natural building materials
- yarn, ribbon, fabric strips
- chopsticks
- plastic strawberry baskets
- modeling clay (optional)
- writing paper

1. Have students use chopsticks as a beak for gathering materials and their hands as claws for weaving.

2. Have children weave a "nest" in the strawberry basket until the inside and outside are covered.

3. The activity may be extended by having students create clay birds and eggs to rest in the "nests."

4. Instruct children to write a "for rent" advertisement for their nest. Display the nests and the advertisements for all to admire.

For Rent
Feather and yarn nest perfect for yellow warbler

Fun Facts

- The mallee fowl of Australia makes a nest 15 feet (4.5 m) high and 35 feet (11.5 m) across.
- The vervain hummingbird builds the smallest nest—about the size of half a walnut!
- Harvester ants can build nests that are 2 feet (60 cm) tall and 2–5 feet (60 cm–150 cm) in diameter.

Creating a Colorful Forest

Trees are divided into two main categories: broadleaf (deciduous) and needleleaf (conifer). *In a Tree* presents an example of both. After reading the book to the class, ask children to guess which tree is the broadleaf and which is the needleleaf. Tell students that they are going to have the opportunity to create their own forest of colorful trees.

DIRECTIONS

MATERIALS

- *In a Tree*
- film canisters
- Fun Foam® (available at craft supply stores)
- scissors
- glue
- ink pads (assorted colors)
- construction paper

1 Draw the children's attention to page 14 of *In a Tree*. Encourage them to look closely at the many colors in the leaves.

2 Place children into small groups of about four or five.

3 Have children make stamps by cutting out tree shapes from the Fun Foam®.

4 Instruct them to glue a shape to the end of each film canister.

5 Encourage children to use the stamps and construction paper to create a colorful forest. Instruct them to share their stamps with other members of their group.

Fun Facts

- The South American milk tree produces a sap that tastes, looks, and can be used just like cow's milk.
- Imagine receiving a wooden postcard. Well, if you were in Canada during the early 1900s you might have, for people often used birch bark as letters and postcards.
- Believe it or not, when you eat cinnamon you are really eating ground up tree bark!

Fruits or Vegetables?

People often mistake fruits for vegetables. For example, a tomato is often thought to be a vegetable, when it is actually a fruit. After reading aloud *In the Garden*, ask students to tell whether each plant in the book is a fruit or a vegetable. Have students explain their answers. Explain that a fruit is the part of a plant that has seeds in it, while a vegetable can be any other part of the plant.

DIRECTIONS

MATERIALS

- *In the Garden*
- pictures of a variety of fruits and vegetables
- Fruits/Vegetables reproducible (page 39)
- crayons or markers
- scissors

1 Distribute pictures of fruits and vegetables, one picture to each student.

2 Name an attribute and ask all students who have a plant with that attribute to stand. For example, when you say *leafy,* all students with pictures of leafy plants should stand.

3 After choosing several attributes, introduce the concept of fruit versus vegetable (a fruit contains the seeds of the plant while a vegetable can be any part of the plant).

4 Have the class divide itself into a fruit group and a vegetable group, based on the picture each student is holding.

5 Distribute the Fruits/Vegetables reproducible and have children color and cut out the pictures to make cards.

6 Have children sort their cards into stacks of vegetables and stacks of fruits.

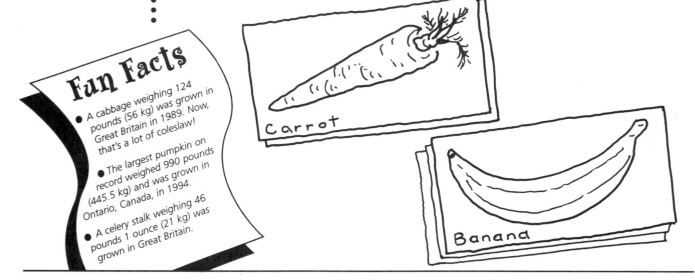

Fun Facts

- A cabbage weighing 124 pounds (56 kg) was grown in Great Britain in 1989. Now, that's a lot of coleslaw!
- The largest pumpkin on record weighed 990 pounds (445.5 kg) and was grown in Ontario, Canada, in 1994.
- A celery stalk weighing 46 pounds 1 ounce (21 kg) was grown in Great Britain.

Carrot

Banana

Fruits/Vegetables

Apple

Watermelon

Celery

Banana

Orange

Carrot

Pumpkin

Lemon

Lettuce

Potato

Mystery Plants

Fruits and vegetables can be sorted in numerous ways, such as by color, size, or weight. We eat many parts of plants and can categorize these as roots, stems, leaves, flowers, fruits, and seeds. After reading aloud *In the Garden*, ask students to sort the pictures in the book based on a particular attribute, for example, according to whether they are plants or animals. Explain that they'll be doing another sorting activity with plants.

DIRECTIONS

MATERIALS

- *In the Garden*
- samples/pictures of various fruits and vegetables
- white butcher paper
- tempera paint
- newspaper
- art supplies
- painted backdrop

1 Ask one person in each pair of students to sort samples or pictures according to an attribute such as color.

2 The other partner should then guess the sorting method.

3 Inform students that the parts of a plant we eat can also be sorted into groups by such attributes as roots, stems, leaves, flowers, fruits, and seeds. Ask students to re-sort the samples/pictures according to what part of the plant they think can be eaten. For example, if the sample is a cherry, they may sort that into the fruit category.

4 Have each pair choose a plant part from the ones discussed and make a "stuffed" fruit or vegetable.

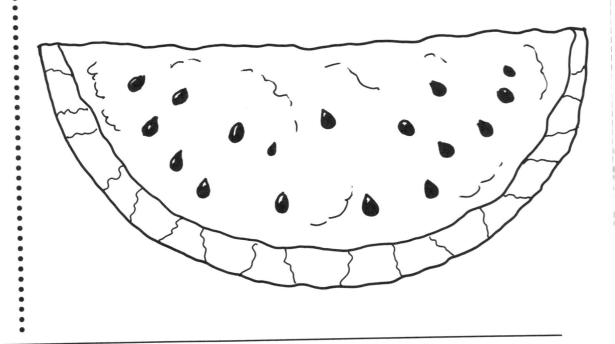

Mystery Plants

5 Distribute two sheets of white butcher paper and invite children to sketch the food item on the top sheet, making it as large as possible.

6 Instruct children to cut out their drawing with the other sheet underneath, creating two identical shapes.

7 Invite children to paint their food with tempera paints.

8 Staple around the edges, leaving a space open to fill the food item with crumpled newspaper. Then, finish stapling and attach it to the appropriate section of a painted backdrop that includes sections for roots, seeds, stems, flowers, fruits, and leaves.

Fun Facts

● According to Guinness, the largest watermelon was grown in Tennessee in 1990 and weighed 262 pounds (109 kg).

● Did you know that many medicines come from plants? Digitalis, a heart medication, is made from Foxglove flowers.

● Botanists have discovered and identified more than 400,000 plants!

Petals

Although petals do not play a direct role in plant reproduction, brightly colored petals attract insects. This attraction aids in pollination. After reading aloud *Among the Flowers*, have children discuss the attributes of the flowers presented in the book, such as color, texture, and shape. Then invite students to sort "the real thing."

DIRECTIONS

MATERIALS

- *Among the Flowers*
- variety of real, silk, and plastic flowers
- index cards
- pencils

1 Display a variety of real, silk, and plastic flowers. Ask children how the flowers could be sorted, such as by those that have thorns versus those that do not.

2 Encourage children to sort and group the flowers and share how they grouped them.

3 Have pairs of students choose one flower and write down four or five attributes on an index card. For example, a student could write *has a scent* or *has thorns*.

4 Have students sit in a circle with all the flowers in the middle.

5 Put the index cards in a pile and have one student select a card and read a clue aloud.

6 After a clue is read, ask the class to guess which flower the attribute card describes. If all guesses are incorrect, invite another student to read the next clue. Continue until all cards have been read.

Fun Facts

- The rose is the national flower of the United States.
- The largest flower in the world is the rafflesia, grown in Southeast Asia. They grow up to 3-feet wide.
- Bouncing Bet is a pretty flower that can be used as soap. Museums use it to clean old lace and tapestries.

1. It has a scent.
2. It has thorns.
3. It is red.

Flower Power

Flowers need pollen to make seeds. *Among the Flowers* presents information on pollination. After reading the book aloud, ask students how pollen gets from one plant to another. Explore the ideas presented in the book, and then direct students in completing the following activity.

DIRECTIONS

MATERIALS

- *Among the Flowers*
- Flower Diagram/Petal Pattern reproducible (page 45)
- cardstock
- scissors
- 4"x 5" pieces of pink, red, orange, or white tissue paper
- pencil
- round doll clothespins
- orange marker or crayon
- yellow pipe cleaners
- masking tape
- green floral tape
- modeling clay
- glue
- talcum powder

1 Using the Flower Diagram/Petal Pattern reproducible, make a petal pattern out of cardstock or tagboard. Have students stack three pieces of tissue paper, trace around the pattern, and cut out all three tissue-paper petals. Then have students stack the petals.

2 Have students roll the curved end of the petal stack around a pencil. They should then create curled edges by pressing the outside edges towards the center. Have students pull out the pencil and separate the three petals.

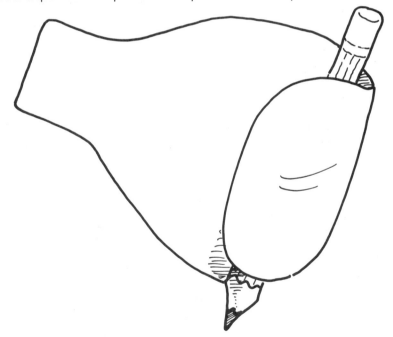

3 Invite students to color the top knob of a doll clothespin with an orange marker or crayon. This will be the pistil.

4 Distribute a pipe cleaner, cut in half, to each student. Have students turn down both ends of each half to make knobs for the top of the stamen. Have them add powder to the "stamen" as pollen.

Flower Power

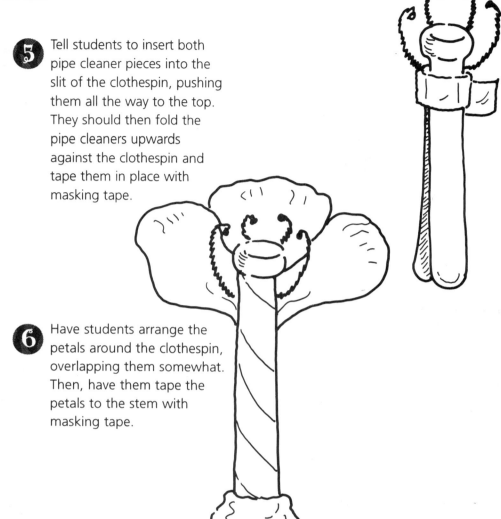

5 Tell students to insert both pipe cleaner pieces into the slit of the clothespin, pushing them all the way to the top. They should then fold the pipe cleaners upwards against the clothespin and tape them in place with masking tape.

6 Have students arrange the petals around the clothespin, overlapping them somewhat. Then, have them tape the petals to the stem with masking tape.

7 Instruct students to wrap the green floral tape over the masking tape all the way down the clothespin.

8 Have students shape a piece of modeling clay around the base to make the flower stand.

9 Distribute the Flower Diagram reproducible and have students color the diagram to match their "flower." Have students fold on the dotted lines and tape the ends together.

Fun Facts

- A water lily found in the Amazon is so large that its leaves can support the weight of a small child.

- The East Indian arum plant relies on the snail to pollinate it. The snail carries the pollen as it crawls up the plant to get the sweet, sticky substance the plant secretes.

- The wild snapdragon is called "Butter and Eggs" because of its coloring.

Flower Diagram

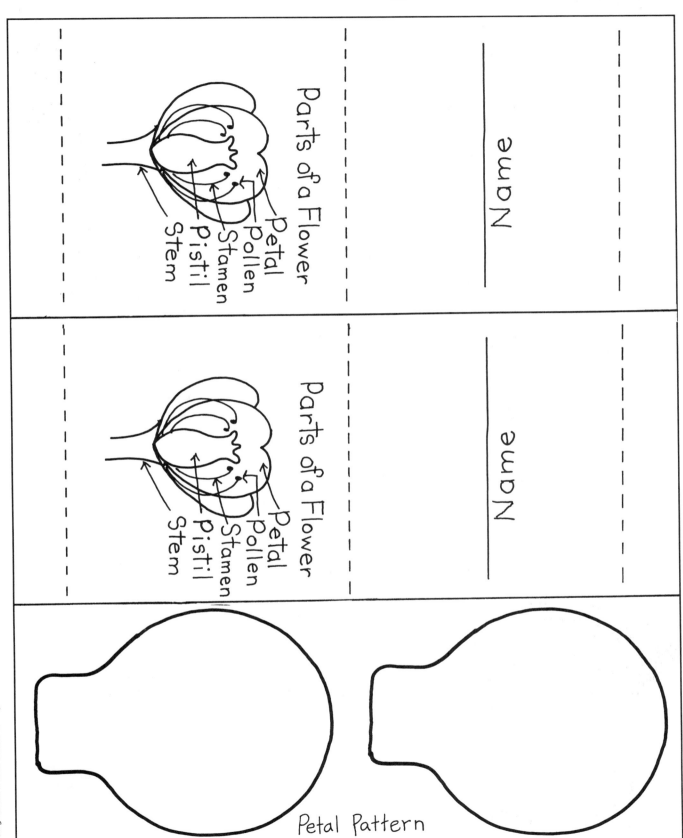

Parts of a Flower

Petal
Pollen
Stamen
Pistil
Stem

Name

Parts of a Flower

Petal
Pollen
Stamen
Pistil
Stem

Name

Petal Pattern

Ants, Ants Everywhere!

Ants, like people, are very "social"—they rely on each other to survive. There are four kinds of ants that work in a colony. Worker ants dig tunnels, tend to the eggs, and look for food. Soldier ants protect the colony. The queen ant lays eggs while the drones, male ants, have the sole job of taking care of the queen. Page 14 of *Underfoot* presents further information about the behavior of ants. Have children discuss observations they've made on their own about ant behavior and then complete the following activity.

DIRECTIONS

MATERIALS

- *Underfoot*
- Ant Colony reproducible (pg. 47)
- crayons
- glue
- 8 ½" x 11" (21 cm x 28 cm) cardboard
- sand
- sesame seeds
- white rice
- minced grass clippings
- pepper
- small plastic ants

1 Invite students to color the grass and rocks on the Ant Colony reproducible and glue the reproducible to the cardboard. Then have students spread glue around the outside of the colony and sprinkle sand on the glue.

2 Instruct the children to glue sesame seeds (eggs) in the hatching room, white rice (larva) next to the seeds, a pinch of grass clippings (food) in the food room and a pinch of pepper (trash) in the trash room.

3 Have students place and glue small plastic ants anywhere on the picture.

4 Encourage students to point to the ants and explain what role they have in a colony, e.g., worker, drone, queen, soldier.

Fun Facts

- There are over 10,000 species of ants!
- Some species of ants can grow as large as 2' 1/2" inches (6.35 cm) long. That's longer than a child's finger.
- Ants often carry loads more than 50 times their own weight! If an 80 pound (36 kg) child could do that, he or she would be able to carry a two-ton truck.

Ant Colony

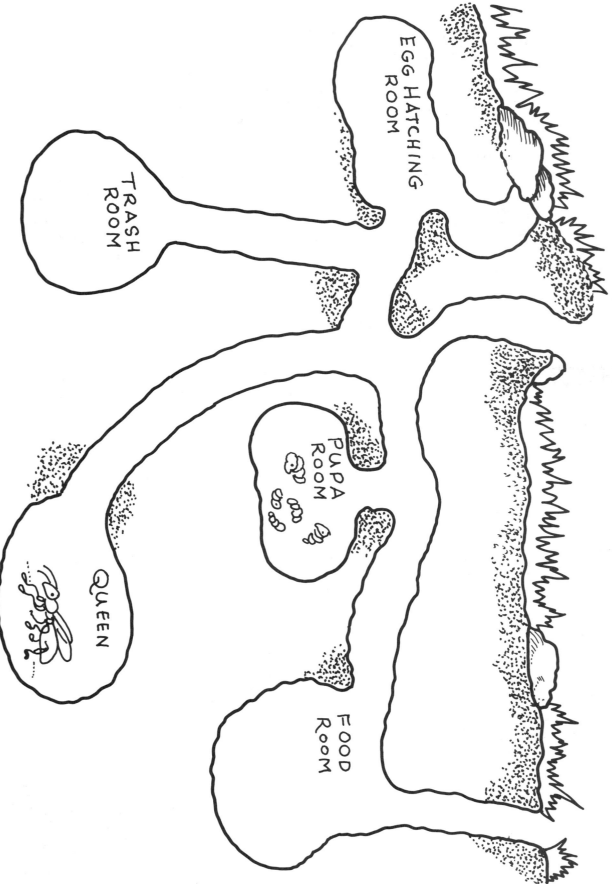

EGG HATCHING ROOM

TRASH ROOM

PUPA ROOM

QUEEN

FOOD ROOM

Exploring Habitats © 1998 Creative Teaching Press

Earthworm Tunnels

Earthworms are fascinating creatures; but because so much of what they do takes place below ground, we rarely get to see their work. Through this experiment, students predict and discover firsthand how earthworms break down, aerate, and fertilize the soil.

DIRECTIONS

MATERIALS

- *Underfoot*
- earthworms (available at a bait shop)
- narrow glass jars
- sand
- moist soil
- little rocks
- black paper
- tape
- science journal

1 Give each student a glass jar and instruct him or her to layer the small rocks on the bottom, followed by alternating layers of sand and moist soil.

2 Have students cover the jars with black paper and tape the paper in place.

3 Give each student a worm to gently place inside the jar.

4 Have students guess what the worms will do and write their predictions in their science journals.

5 Instruct students to leave the paper on the jar for seven days. Then, have students review their science journal notes. Invite students to remove the paper and discuss their findings. Have students write their findings in their science journal.

Fun Facts

- Did you ever wonder why worms come out in the rain? Worms breathe through their skin and if their tunnels fill up with rain, they drown.

- Imagine the thoughts of the lucky bird in Transvaal, South Africa, who found the longest worm in the world. It measured 22 feet (6.6 m)!

- There are 20,000 different kinds of worms!

The Case of the Different Antennae

Many insects feel, smell, and taste with their antennae. However, not all antennae are the same. Antennae may be long, short, thin, fat, segmented, or feathery. Through this activity, your "detectives" will get a chance to look at the antennae of various insects as well as make a set of antennae modeled after one insect.

DIRECTIONS

MATERIALS

- 1 ½" x 9" (4 cm x 23 cm) posterboard
- hole punch
- pipe cleaners
- bump chenille pipe cleaners
- small macaroni pieces
- masking tape
- 12" (30.5 cm) yarn
- Detective Log (page 51)

1 Divide the class into small "detective agency" groups. Invite each detective agency to examine a *Look Once, Look Again* book and observe photographs of insects and their antennae.

2 Rotate the books among the groups until each detective agency has seen all the books.

3 Ask each student to draw a picture and write a short description of the antennae for each insect listed on the Detective Log.

4 Assign an insect to each detective agency: butterfly, ant, moth, dragonfly, and grasshopper.

The Case of the Different Antennae

5 Ask each agency to "use the clues" from the detective logs and follow these directions to make pipe-cleaner antennae for its assigned insect.

Butterfly—Fold the ends of two pieces of pipe cleaner to form knobs.

Ant—Fold each of two pipe cleaners into an "L" shape.

Moth—Twist two pieces of bump chenille around the ends of two pipe cleaners.

Dragonfly/Grasshopper—Bend the top of the pipe cleaners enough so that the macaroni pieces won't fall off. Add macaroni pieces over the pipe cleaner until they almost reach the top.

Mosquito—Use two bump chenille pieces.

Beetle—Twist two pieces of pipe cleaner together, making one end fatter than the other. Repeat for second set of pipe cleaners. Bend the tops slightly.

6 Have each student fit a sentence strip to his or her head as a headband, tape the strip in place, and tape the antennae to the front of the headband. Have students label the sentence strip with the name of the insect.

Fun Facts

● Long Horn Beetles may have antennae that are two to four times their body length.

● Male mosquitoes use their antennae to detect females up to 1/4 mile (0.4 km) away.

● Flies taste with their feet instead of with their antennae.

The Case of the Different Antennae

Name _____   Date _____

Moth

_____

_____

Grasshopper

_____

_____

Butterfly

_____

_____

Ant

_____

_____

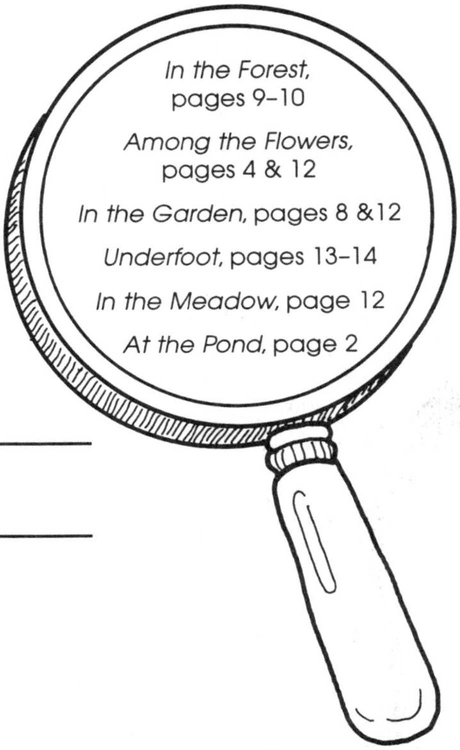

In the Forest,
pages 9–10

Among the Flowers,
pages 4 & 12

In the Garden, pages 8 & 12

Underfoot, pages 13–14

In the Meadow, page 12

At the Pond, page 2

Dragonfly

_____

_____

The Case of the Mysterious Smells

Many animals have a keen sense of smell. After reading aloud the *Look Once, Look Again* books, have children name the pictured animals that can smell very well. Smell is the most ancient sense. Scientists divide all smells into six main types: fruity, flowery, spicy, bad, burned, and resinous (like tree sap). Encourage your "detectives" to use their noses to gather clues to the identities of the mysterious smells.

DIRECTIONS

MATERIALS

- film canisters
- cotton balls
- assorted extracts (chocolate, mint, vanilla)
- rubbing alcohol
- vinegar
- spices (cinnamon, nutmeg, cumin)
- coffee
- peanut butter
- Detective Log (page 53)

1 Number all canisters.

2 For all liquids, insert a cotton ball into each canister being used. Add a few drops of the liquid and close the container. Place solid materials, such as spices, coffee, and peanut butter, directly into the container and place a cotton ball on top of the material to hide it.

3 Teach children how to carefully smell the odors. Explain that they should open the container part way and sniff close to, but not right on top of, the opening.

4 Have children sniff a container and write down their guess in their detective logs. Encourage children to remember where they might have smelled the scent before. Continue until all containers have been sniffed.

5 Disclose the identity of what's in each container and have students compare their guesses with the actual substance. Discuss how these substances are used in daily life.

Fun Facts

- Certain male moths can smell female moths up to several miles away!
- Armadillos have a very good sense of smell. They can even smell insects living nearly a foot underground.
- An elephant's trunk is actually a nose and an upper lip combined. The elephant does most of its breathing through its trunk.

The Case of the Mysterious Smells

Name

Date

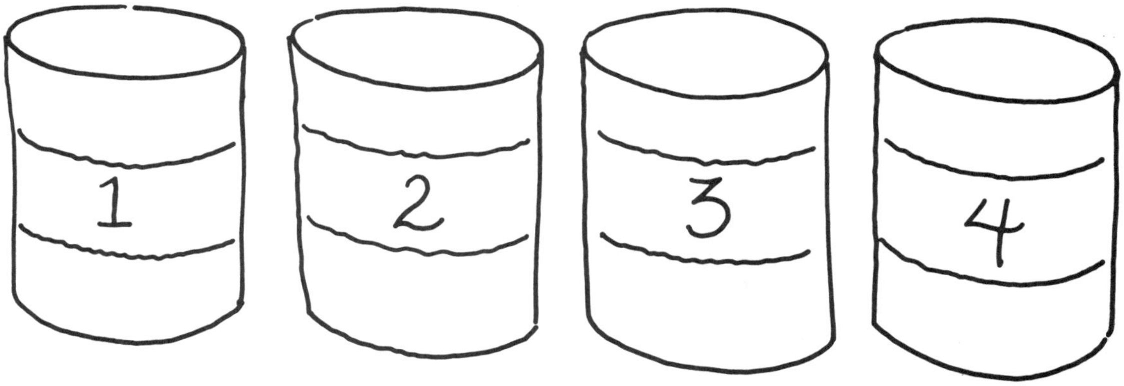

1   2   3   4

My Guess   _____ _____ _____ _____

Actual
Item   _____ _____ _____ _____

Place the smells in order from the one you liked the best to the one you liked the least.

_____ _____ _____ _____

liked the best   liked the least

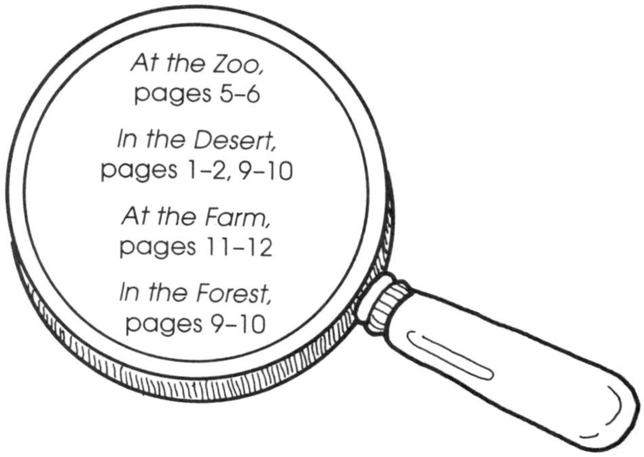

At the Zoo,
pages 5–6

In the Desert,
pages 1–2, 9–10

At the Farm,
pages 11–12

In the Forest,
pages 9–10

The Secret of Plant Protection

Like animals, plants need protection from environmental factors and predators. Many plants have special features that help them survive. For example, evergreens have small needle-like leaves that allow snow to slide off. Cactus plants must survive on very little water. Their "leaves" are thin spikes so that less water is lost through transpiration. In addition, these spines deter predators. Encourage students to examine the pictures in the *Look Once, Look Again* books and suggest ways plants protect themselves.

DIRECTIONS

MATERIALS

- craft items
- scissors
- glue
- tape
- Detective Log (page 55)

1 Have students brainstorm ways animals protect themselves from predators, such as through claws, teeth, venom, speed, odor, and camouflage. Explain that plants also have ways to defend themselves.

2 Brainstorm the reasons plants protect themselves.

3 Share the pages listed on the Detective Log and suggest that children use their detective instincts to discover how each plant protects itself. Have them list the defense mechanisms in their Detective Log.

4 Divide the class into pairs and have each pair use craft items, scissors, glue, tape, and their imaginations to invent plants with novel defense mechanisms. Have children draw a picture of their plant and describe in their Detective Log how their plant protects itself.

5 Invite students to share their creations with the class.

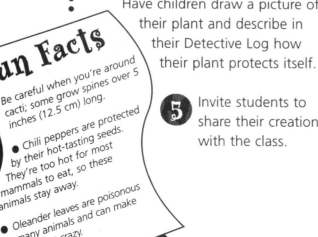

Fun Facts

- Be careful when you're around cacti; some grow spines over 5 inches (12.5 cm) long.

- Chili peppers are protected by their hot-tasting seeds. They're too hot for most mammals to eat, so these animals stay away.

- Oleander leaves are poisonous to many animals and can make horses act crazy.

The Secret of Plant Protection

_____   _____
Name   Date

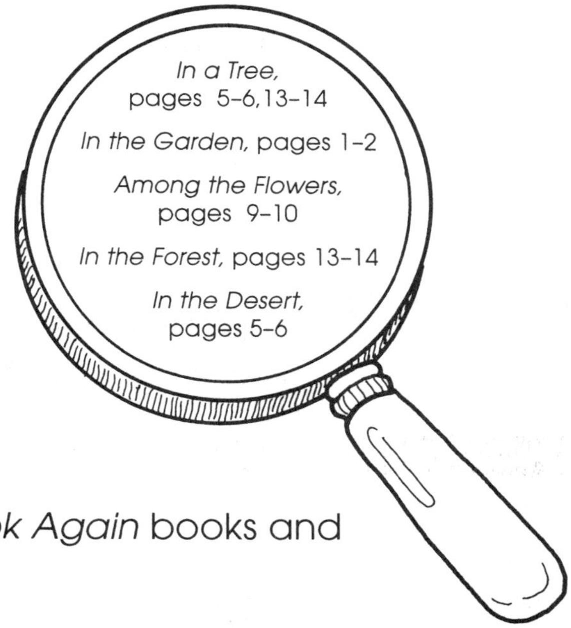

Reasons plants protect themselves

1._____

_____

2._____

_____

In a Tree,
pages 5–6, 13–14

In the Garden, pages 1–2

Among the Flowers,
pages 9–10

In the Forest, pages 13–14

In the Desert,
pages 5–6

Here are three plants from the _Look Once, Look Again_ books and the ways they protect themselves.

1. _____   _____
   plant name

2. _____   _____
   plant name

3. _____   _____
   plant name

Here is a picture of my plant.

This is how my plant protects itself.

_____

_____

_____

_____

_____

Play the Animal Protection Game

In the *Look Once, Look Again* books, many animals are presented that protect themselves in a number of ways—some hide, while others use their sharp teeth or claws. In this modified version of tag, children will learn how different animals protect themselves.

DIRECTIONS

MATERIALS

- 2 sets of laminated "protection" signs with the following phrases:

  Horns or Antlers

  Sharp Teeth and Claws

  Ability to Get Away

  Camouflage for Hiding

  Special Features

- animal name cards—the animals found in the *Look Once, Look Again* books

- Detective Log (page 58)

1 Have each detective agency look through the books, choose four animals, and use the chart on the Detective Log to note how the animals pictured protect themselves. Set these notes aside.

2 Go to the gym or playground. Draw two parallel lines about 40 feet apart.

3 Tape a set of "protection" signs to the walls behind both lines.

4 Have students stand on one of the lines. Give each child an animal name card.

5 Choose a "predator," who stands between the two lines.

6 When the predator says *Go,* the "animals" run from where they are standing to the other line. The goal is to place themselves in a group marked with the sign that represents how they would protect themselves. For example, a zebra may run to the area marked *Camouflage for Hiding* or the area labeled *Ability to Get Away.*

Play the Animal Protection Game

7 The predator tries to catch one of the animals before it gets to its sign. (Every animal caught joins the predator in the middle and becomes a new predator.)

8 Have the children run once again to the other line and stand in the area marked with a sign that indicates their method of protection. Animals who have only one protective mechanism run to the area that is labeled the same as the one in which they are currently standing.

9 Continue the game until everyone is caught.

10 Discuss where they chose to stand and what happens once predators outnumber the prey.

11 Redistribute the cards and play again.

12 Return to the classroom. Have students list their observations on the Detective Log.

Fun Facts

- If a sea cucumber is attacked, it throws up its insides. This tends to stop the attacker. After a few weeks, the insides grow back.
- If a horned lizard wants to scare off an enemy, it squirts blood from the edges of its lower eyelids.
- When toads are in trouble, they may trick their enemy by puffing themselves up with air. This way, they look bigger than they actually are.

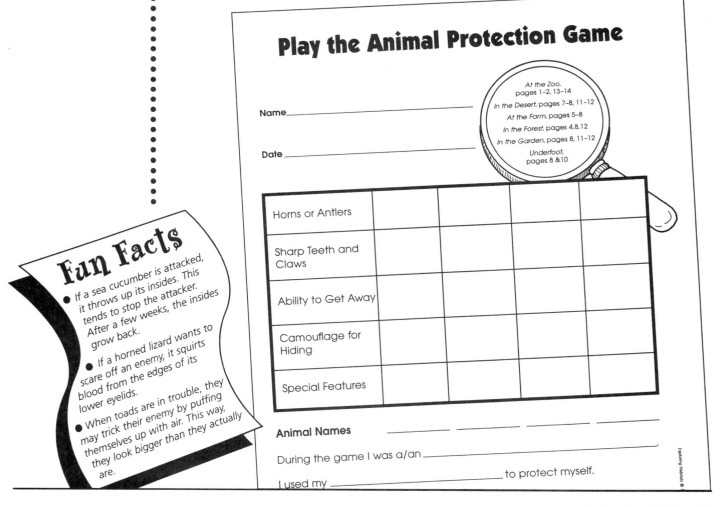

Play the Animal Protection Game

At the Zoo, pages 1–2, 13–14
In the Desert, pages 7–8, 11–12
At the Farm, pages 5–8
In the Forest, pages 4, 8, 12
In the Garden, pages 8, 11–12
Underfoot, pages 8 & 10

Name_____

Date_____

Horns or Antlers				
Sharp Teeth and Claws				
Ability to Get Away				
Camouflage for Hiding				
Special Features				

Animal Names _____ _____ _____

During the game I was a/an _____

I used my _____ to protect myself.

Play the Animal Protection Game

Name_____

Date_____

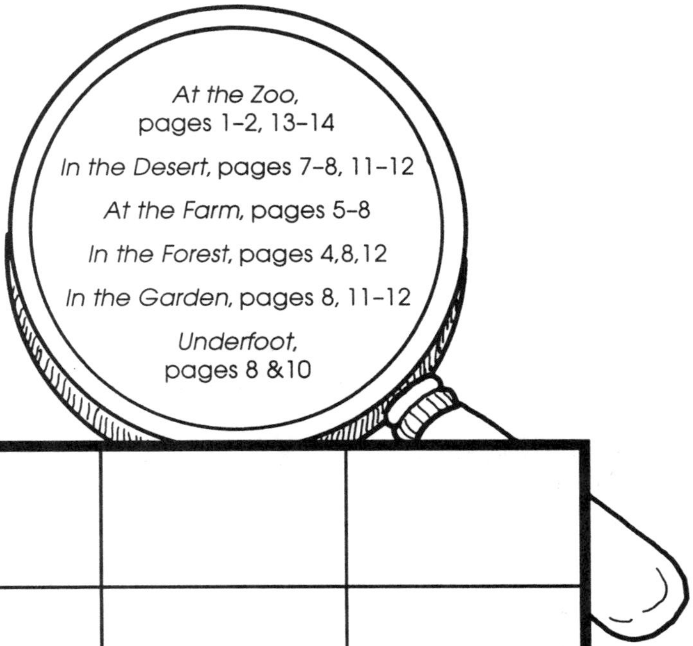

At the Zoo,
pages 1–2, 13–14

In the Desert, pages 7–8, 11–12

At the Farm, pages 5–8

In the Forest, pages 4,8,12

In the Garden, pages 8, 11–12

Underfoot,
pages 8 &10

Horns or Antlers				
Sharp Teeth and Claws				
Ability to Get Away				
Camouflage for Hiding				
Special Features				

Animal Names   _____ _____ _____ _____

During the game I was a/an _____.

I used my _____ to protect myself.

When there were a lot of predators I _____

_____.

Exploring Habitats © 1998 Creative Teaching Press

Feet Fossils

The shape and design of an animal's legs and feet help it move. Animals with webbed feet need them for living in or near water. Those with longer claws on their feet use them for fighting, clinging, or grasping. Animals with hooves often live where the ground is rocky. In this activity, each detective agency will create its own footprint fossils.

DIRECTIONS

MATERIALS

- modeling clay
- plaster of paris
- Detective Log (page 60)

1 Share with the children the pictures of different animal feet found in the *Look Once, Look Again* books. Have children find examples of animals with feet that are used for digging, walking, jumping, swimming, and grasping.

2 Have children draw an example of each type of foot.

3 Have each detective agency choose one of the animals.

4 Give each agency modeling clay and instruct the members to make a mold of the type of foot they have chosen.

5 Instruct the students to pour plaster of paris into the molds and let it dry.

6 Have students write in their Detective Logs what they learned from this activity.

Fun Facts

- An ostrich can't fly, but its long legs help it run up to 40 miles an hour!
- Porcupines, bears, raccoons, and squirrels walk on flat feet. Foxes, moose, cows, and sheep walk on their tiptoes.
- Swans have large, webbed paddles for feet. When they get too hot, the webs get sweaty.

Feet Fossils

☐ digging	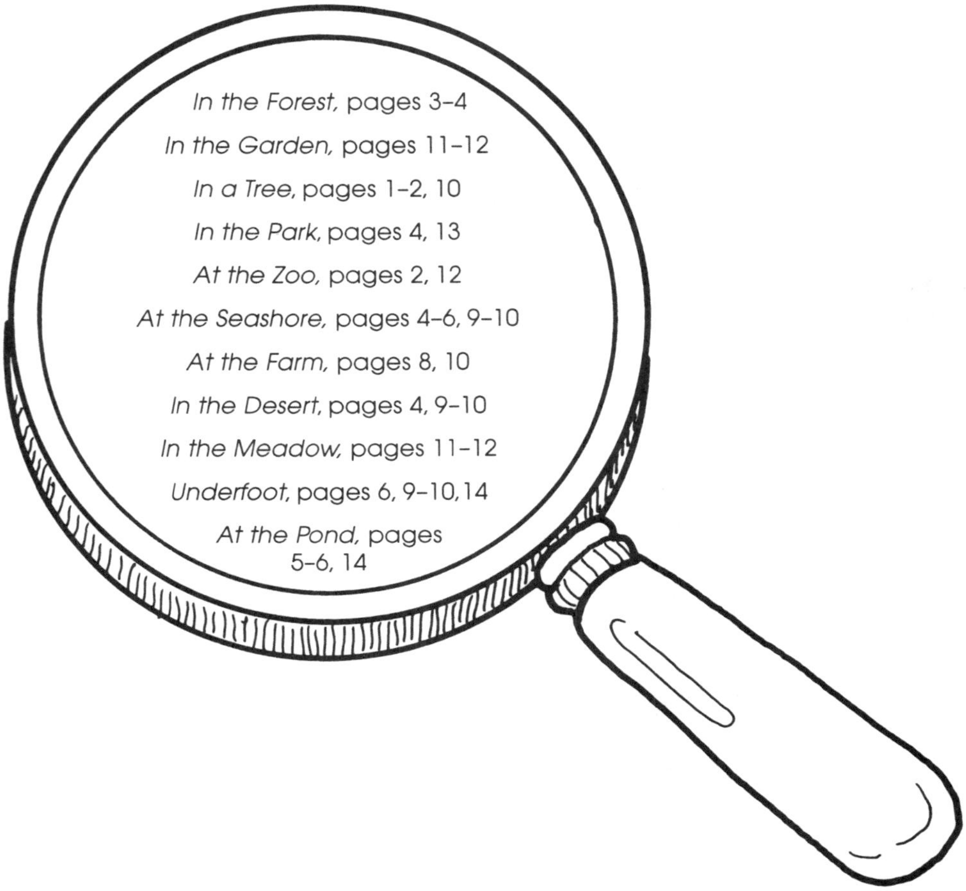 *In the Forest,* pages 3–4
	In the Garden, pages 11–12
	In a Tree, pages 1–2, 10
	In the Park, pages 4, 13
☐ walking	*At the Zoo,* pages 2, 12
	At the Seashore, pages 4–6, 9–10
	At the Farm, pages 8, 10
	In the Desert, pages 4, 9–10
	In the Meadow, pages 11–12
	Underfoot, pages 6, 9–10, 14
	At the Pond, pages 5–6, 14

☐ jumping   ☐ swimming   ☐ grasping

My observations from the activity

_____

_____

Exploring Habitats © 1998 Creative Teaching Press

Mysterious Seeds

Although most children know that seeds produce plants, many do not know the three parts of a seed. The *seed coat* covers and protects the seed until conditions are right for germination. The bulk of the seed is actually stored *food*. The baby plant will use this until it grows leaves and can produce food through photosynthesis. Finally, there is the baby plant inside a seed called the *embryo*. Have your detectives investigate the parts of a seed.

DIRECTIONS

MATERIALS

- ½ bag dry lima beans
- medium- or large-size bowl and water
- paper towels
- patterns for seed parts
- 9" x 12" (23 cm x 30.5 cm) construction paper
- Seed Parts reproducibles (pages 63–64)
- scissors
- glue
- black marker
- Detective Log (page 65)

1 Put lima beans in a bowl and cover with water. Let beans soak overnight.

2 Reproduce the seed coat pattern on brown paper, the baby plant pattern on green paper, and the food part of the seed on white paper.

3 Discuss the function of a seed. Ask students what they think a seed is like inside. Have them draw a picture of their hypothesis in their Detective Logs.

4 Demonstrate how to remove the seed coat by gently rubbing a lima bean seed between the thumb and forefinger. Show how to open the seed with gentle pressure.

Mysterious Seeds

5 Ask children to guess which part is the baby plant. Then explain that the bulk of the seed is actually the food for the baby plant. Encourage students to find the parts of a seed using their own seed.

6 Instruct children to cut out each of the parts on the Seed Parts reproducibles.

7 Have students glue the seed parts in the following order:
    a. Glue the Food to the Seed Coat.
    b. Glue the Baby Plant to the dotted line on top of the Food.
    c. Fold the seed on the dotted line to make a book.
    d. Glue the Seed Coat title to the front cover of the seed book.

8 Have students draw a picture of how the inside of the seed actually looked to complete their Detective Log.

Fun Facts

- The seed of a double coconut tree can weigh as much as 44 pounds (20 kg). That's about the same as a first grade student weighs.
- The South African national flower, the protea, will germinate only after being scorched by a fire.
- The seeds of a tobacco plant are so small that 2,500 may grow in a pod that is less than ³/₄ inch (19 m) long.

Seed Parts #1

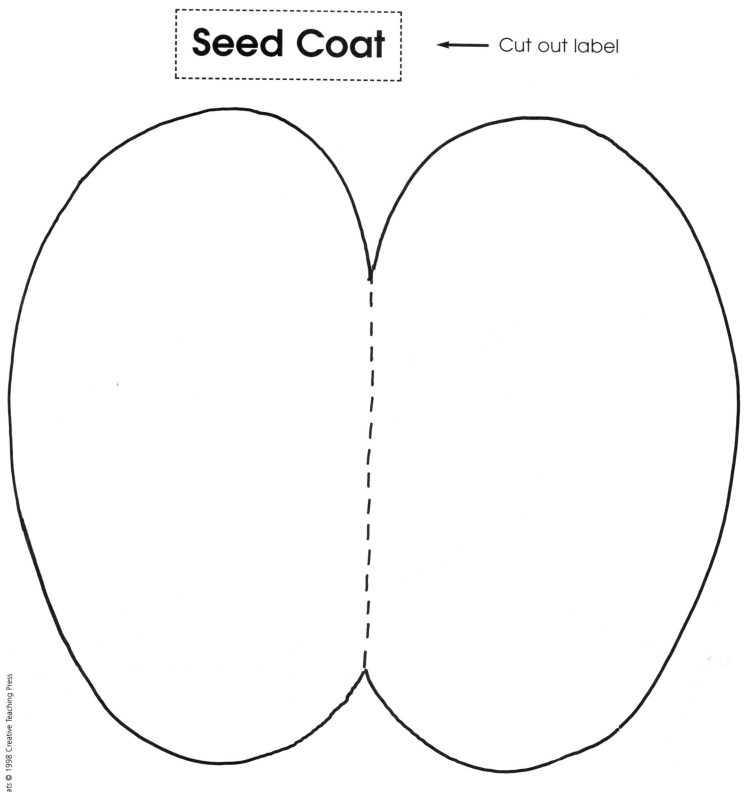

Seed Coat ← Cut out label

Cut on solid lines.

Seed Parts #2

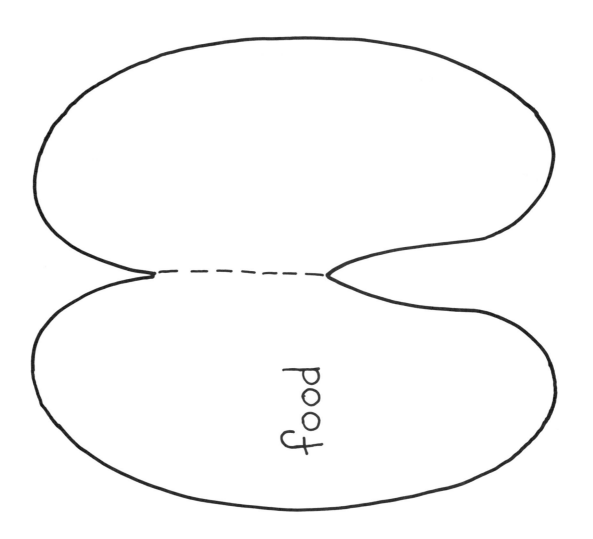

food

Baby Plant

Exploring Habitats © 1998 Creative Teaching Press

Mysterious Seeds

Name _____   Date _____

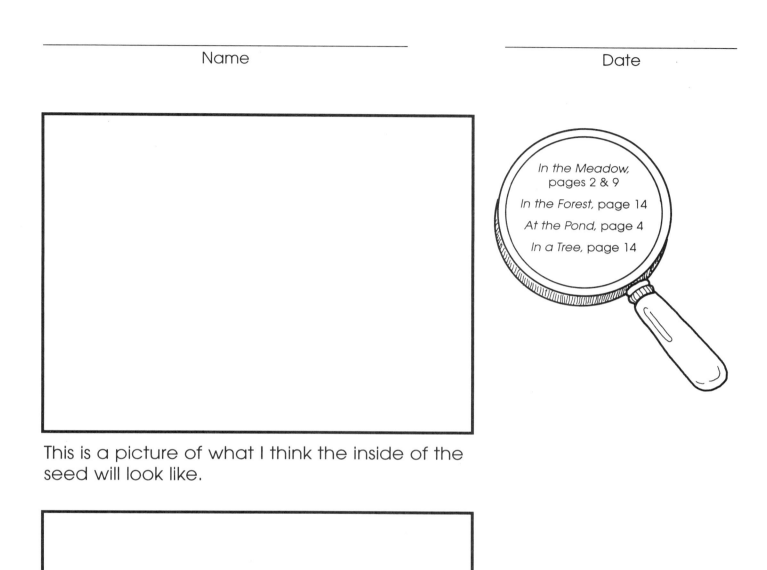

In the Meadow, pages 2 & 9

In the Forest, page 14

At the Pond, page 4

In a Tree, page 14

This is a picture of what I think the inside of the seed will look like.

This is a picture of how the seed actually looked.

The Mystery of the Traveling Seeds

Seeds have a better chance of growing if they do not try to live right next to the mother plant. If seeds only fell to the ground around the mother plant, there would be too many seedlings together, and none of them would have enough nutrients to grow successfully. So, plants have developed some interesting adaptations to help their seeds travel to a new location. Three of the ways that seeds travel are by wind, water, and "hitchhiking." Have your students investigate the ways in which seeds travel.

DIRECTIONS

MATERIALS

- clay
- craft items (drinking straws, yarn, toothpicks, cellophane tape)
- scissors
- tape
- stuffed animals
- bucket of water
- stopwatches
- rulers
- Detective Log (page 68)

1 Discuss with students the importance of seed dispersal for plant survival. Brainstorm ideas about how seeds could possibly travel by wind, water, and animals.

2 Instruct students to write their ideas of what will work to move a seed. Ask them to predict methods that will work and write these methods in their Detective Log.

The Mystery of the Traveling Seeds

_____   _____
Name   Date

These are three ways that seeds are dispersed.

1._____

2._____

3._____

I predict that I'll be able to move a seed by

_____

Here is a picture of how I helped my seed travel.

In the Park, pages 4, 9–10
In a Tree, page 2
In the Forest, page 2
In the Garden, pages 5–6, 9–10
Among the Flowers, pages 1–2
In the Meadow, pages 9–10

The Mystery of the Traveling Seeds

3 Have students attach craft items to pea-size clay ball "seeds" so the items can float, parachute, or "hitchhike," thereby simulating seed dispersal.

4 Take students outside to test their creations. Invite them to time how long seeds cling to stuffed animals or float in a bucket of water. Students can use rulers to measure how far a seed can parachute in the air.

5 Encourage students to discuss their observations and write the outcomes in their Detective Log.

Fun Facts

- Some seeds have been reported to travel up to 32 miles (50 km) in strong winds.

- The seeds of mistletoe plants are unique in that they must land on a tree. If they fall to the ground, they die.

- Some plants burst open, sending their seeds flying. The mountain wisteria shoots its seeds up to 17' (5 m) away.

The Mystery of the Traveling Seeds

_____   _____
          Name   Date

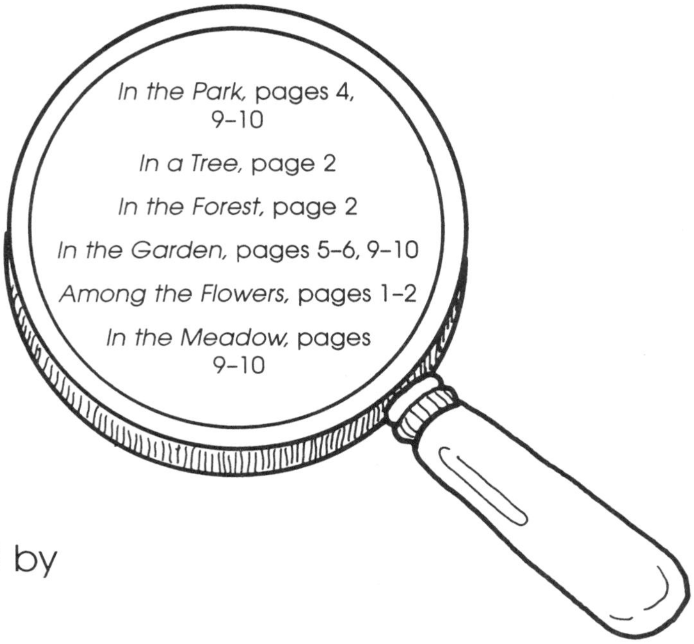

These are three ways that seeds are dispersed.

1._____

2._____

3._____

In the Park, pages 4, 9–10

In a Tree, page 2

In the Forest, page 2

In the Garden, pages 5–6, 9–10

Among the Flowers, pages 1–2

In the Meadow, pages 9–10

I predict that I'll be able to move a seed by

_____.

Here is a picture of how I helped my seed travel.

Exploring Habitats © 1998 Creative Teaching Press

The Case of the Missing Teeth

Teeth tell a lot about an animal. Herbivores, plant-eating animals, have flat incisors and round molars. Carnivores, meat-eating animals, have sharp canines and pointed molars. Omnivores, animals that eat both meat and plants, have incisors, canines, and molars. Human adults (omnivores) have an additional type of tooth called premolars. The following activity invites students to explore their own teeth.

DIRECTIONS

MATERIALS

- small mirrors
- four colors of crayons
- Teeth Chart reproducible (page 71)
- Detective Log (page 72)

1 Share the teeth pictures from the *Look Once, Look Again* books. Encourage students to examine the teeth of the animals and draw their observations on the Detective Log.

2 Explain that different teeth are used for different foods. For example, incisors are used for biting and molars are used for chewing. Canine teeth are used for grasping and tearing food.

3 Distribute the Teeth Chart reproducible.

4 Have children color each type of tooth a different color.

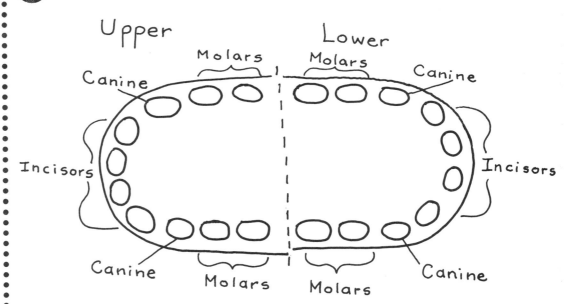

The Case of the Missing Teeth

5 Distribute small mirrors to pairs of students. Instruct the children to examine their teeth and to notice if they are all the same or if some are different. Ask them to count their teeth. Partners can help each other.

6 Ask partners to help each other graph the number they have of each kind of tooth.

7 Have children complete the Detective Log.

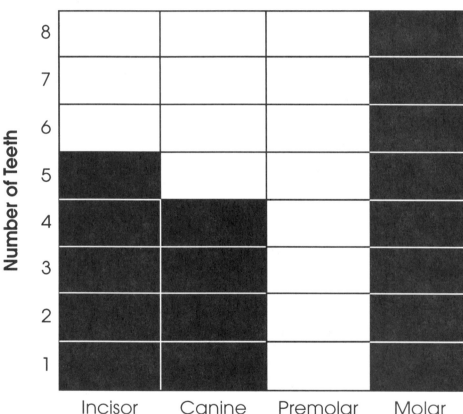

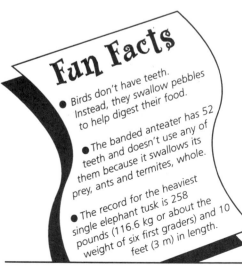

Fun Facts

● Birds don't have teeth. Instead, they swallow pebbles to help digest their food.

● The banded anteater has 52 teeth and doesn't use any of them because it swallows its prey, ants and termites, whole.

● The record for the heaviest single elephant tusk is 258 pounds (116.6 kg or about the weight of six first graders) and 10 feet (3 m) in length.

Teeth Chart

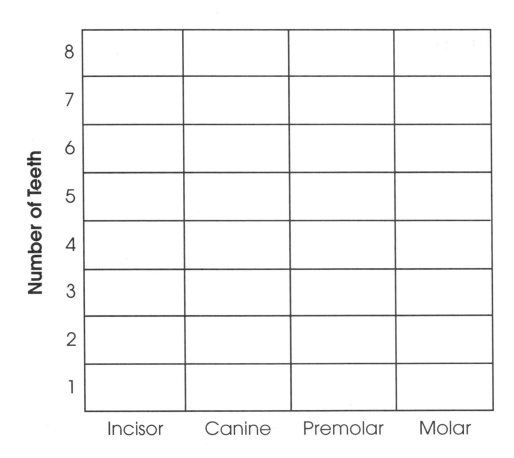

Number of Teeth

8 7 6 5 4 3 2 1

Incisor   Canine   Premolar   Molar

Primary Teeth Pattern

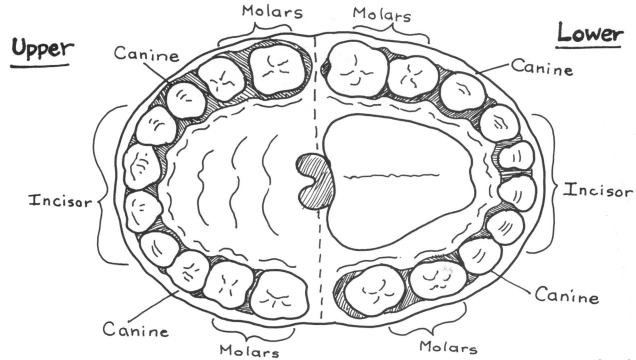

Molars   Molars

Upper   Canine   Lower

Canine

Incisor   Incisor

Canine

Canine   Canine

Molars   Molars

The Case of the Missing Teeth

_____   _____
        Name   Date

[ ]

The mouse's
teeth look
like this.

In the Park, pages 3-4
At the Zoo page 8
At the Farm pages 5-6

[ ]

My teeth look
like this.

I predict that I have _____ teeth altogether.

I predict that I have _____ incisors _____ molars

_____ canines _____ premolars

I actually have _____ incisors _____ molars

_____ canines _____ premolars

Exploring Habitats © 1998 Creative Teaching Press

Guess Who's Coming to Lunch

Birds have customized beaks to help them eat specific foods. For example, the eagle has a beak designed to help it eat meat. A cardinal has a beak for cracking nuts. Bird beaks come in a variety of shapes and sizes. After reviewing the pages in several *Look Once, Look Again* books, ask children to discuss their observations and complete the following activity.

DIRECTIONS

MATERIALS

Tools

- clothespin (grasping-type beak)
- spoon (scooping-type beak)
- chopsticks or needle-nose pliers (probing-type beak)
- craft stick (shovel-type beak)

Food

- marbles (snails)
- Gummy Worms (worms)
- dry beans (pill bugs)
- sunflower seeds (seeds)
- pie tin
- small cups
- Detective Log (page 74)

1 Form groups by detective agencies. Have students read and answer the top portion of the Detective Log.

2 Instruct students to choose a bird from the books to role-play and select the tool that represents its type of beak. Explain that they will pretend that a cup is the bird's stomach and try to pick up as much food as possible using the beaks.

3 Have students pour the food into the pie tin. Explain that when you say *Go* they will have 30 seconds to "eat" as much food as they can by using the "beak" and picking up the pieces of food. Dropped pieces must be returned to the tin.

4 After 30 seconds, have students count the number of pieces in their cup.

5 Discuss observations, such as beaks that made it easier to pick up a certain type of food, and have the students match these in the Detective Log.

Fun Facts

- The bird with the longest bill in relationship to body size is the swordbilled hummingbird.

- Can you imagine having to eat your breakfast while standing on your head? Flamingos can eat only with their heads upside down.

- Bird beaks continue to grow. Eating food helps wear them down.

Guess Who's Coming to Lunch

Name _____   Date _____

I predict the grasping beak will best pick up the _____

I predict the probing beak will best pick up the _____

I predict the scooping beak will best pick up the _____

I predict the shovel beak will best pick up the _____

I think I will pick up _____ pieces of food.

In a Tree, pages 4, 12

In the Park, pages 6, 11–12

At the Farm, pages 4, 13–14

Among the Flowers, pages 7–8

At the Seashore, pages 3–4

At the Zoo, pages 4, 11–12

At the Pond, page 10

For each food, match the beak that picked it up best.

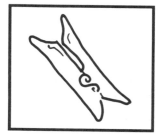  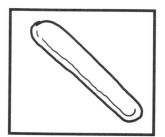 

Exploring Habitats © 1998 Creative Teaching Press

Wrap It Up Activities

Wrap It up is a collection of activities to use as a review, an assessment, or a culmination. This list is designed to be used in conjunction with the animal and plant pictures on pages 77–80. These fantastic illustrations are based on the same pictures found in the *Look Once, Look Again* books. Share these ideas with your students and watch their eyes light up with enjoyment!

1 Place all animal pictures (pages 77–79) in a bag (enough for one per student). Invite each student to draw one picture from the bag and then
- design a perfect habitat for it.
- list five of its characteristics.

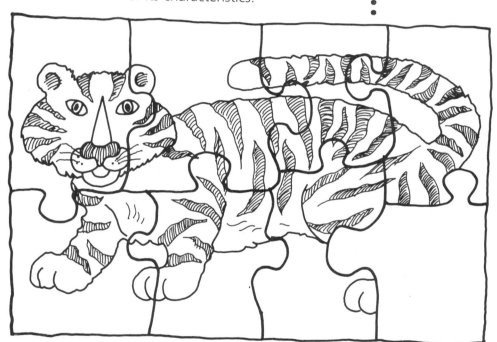

- list ways it is the same or different from himself or herself.
- create a story around the character (choose more than one character).
- describe a day-in-the-life of that creature.
- create a three-panel cartoon strip.
- write a four-line rhyme about that creature.
- design a "Save the _____" poster encouraging wildlife preservation.

- research basic information and make a "fact catcher."
- create a puppet and act out a one-act play.
- write a riddle for that creature on a pop-up book.
- create a lost-and-found advertisement for that creature.
- paint a picture of the animal; then cut it into a puzzle.
- create a shape book with a story about the creature.
- design a paper bag vest that highlights the animal's features.

2 Reproduce a double set of the picture cards (pages 77–80). Laminate them and cut them apart. Invite students to play these card games using the pictures:
- Concentration
- Rummy

3 Give each group of students a set of picture cards (77–80) to sort and classify by
- habitat
- vertebrate/invertebrate
- plant/animal
- number of legs
- amphibian, reptile, bird, fish, mammal

4 Create a blank bingo card. Then have each student place one animal picture in each space to create a unique BINGO card. Call out a fact about each animal related to where it lives or how it looks (or use a fun fact). Students cover a square if the fact matches an animal on their card.

5 Map
- the continent or country where each animal is found in its natural habitat.
- a zoo that includes exhibits for each habitat.

6 Have small groups create a mural for their habitat and then
- draw the corresponding animals to go with it.
- create a passport page for each habitat of the *Look Once, Look Again* books. Have students move from group to group obtaining stamps for each habitat.
- use recyclable materials to make "life-size" replicas of their animal.
- make a quilt with squares highlighting each of the animals.

7 Instruct the students to use the fun facts and then
- create a time line using the dates.
- paint a picture of a fun fact.
- write and design a newspaper using the fun facts as story ideas.

- create a quiz game to be played by the other students.
- make a game board that incorporates those facts.

8 Pair students. Have each student draw an animal card (pages 77–79) from the bag and then
- create a Venn diagram comparing the two.
- create a skit with the two animals as the main characters.
- write an interview between the characters.
- have them be pen pals and write a letter to each other.

9 Graph
- the animal liked best by the class.
- the number of animals pictured for each habitat.
- the number of legs on each animal.
- the number of amphibians, reptiles, fish, birds, mammals.

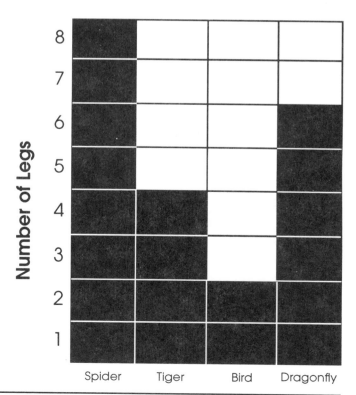

Animals

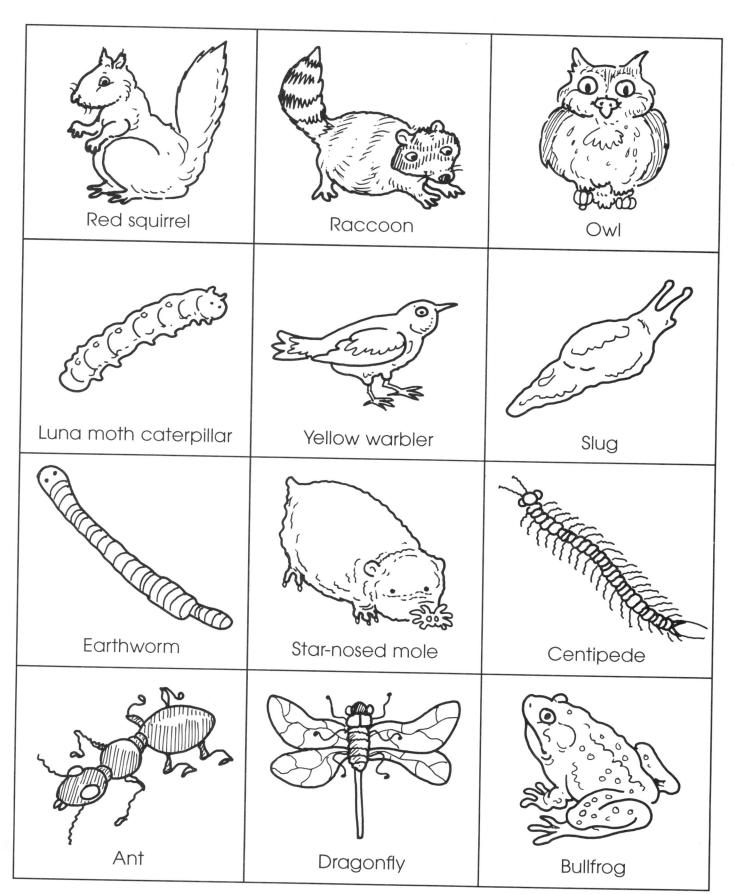

Red squirrel

Raccoon

Owl

Luna moth caterpillar

Yellow warbler

Slug

Earthworm

Star-nosed mole

Centipede

Ant

Dragonfly

Bullfrog

Animals

Snapping turtle

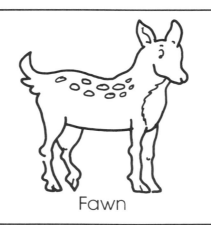

Fawn

Red fox

Green Snake

Pigeon

Swan

Cottontail rabbit

Tiger

Peacock

Lion

Elephant

Camel

Animals

Parrot	Zebra	Sheep
Rooster	Mouse	Goat
Horse	Pig	Crab
Sea star	Tarantula	Scorpion

Plants

Fern

Oak tree

Potato

Peas

Strawberry

Pumpkin

Cactus

Sunflower

Bleeding heart

Rose

Daylily

Seaweed

Exploring Habitats © 1998 Creative Teaching Press